DROP

T H E

ROCK

DROP THE ROCK

REMOVING CHARACTER DEFECTS

Bill Pittman • Todd Weber

 HAZELDEN®

INFORMATION & EDUCATIONAL SERVICES

Copyright ©1993 Hazelden Foundation
Previously Published by Glen Abbey Books, Inc.
First published 1999 by Hazelden
All rights reserved.

Published by Hazelden
Center City, MN
1-800-328-9000
www.hazelden.org

Cover design by
Graphiti Associates, Inc.
Seattle, Washington

Library of Congress
Cataloging-in-Publication Data

Pittman, Bill / Weber, Todd
    Drop the rock : removing character
defects / by Bill Pittman. -- 1st ed.
            p.   cm.
    1.   Personality disorders--Patients--
Rehabilitation. 2. Twelve-step programs.
3. Self-help techniques. I. Title.
    RC554.P57 1992   92-4263
    158'.1--dc20   CIP

First Edition
ISBN 1-56838-504-8
Printed in the United States of America

10 9 8 7

Dedicated to
the Good Works of
FRANKLIN BERGER
LARRY BARNETT
and all those
involved with
THE NEW YORK HAZELDEN
ALUMNI ASSOCIATION
and
HAZELDEN FELLOWSHIP CLUB
NEW YORK

ACKNOWLEDGMENTS

We wish to express our gratitude
to all those individuals in
12 Step Programs who
helped us complete this work.
Our thanks to the following individuals
who allowed us to use their stories:
Mary, Mike, Deb, Karen, Charlie, Pat,
Richard, Lisa, Betty, Judith, Pam,
Peter, Joe, Joan, Sam, John, Nancy,
Erin, Frank, Curtis, Gail,
Stephen, and Bob.

A special thank you
to our manuscript readers
for their valuable comments:
Peter L., Waltham, MA;
Deb M., Pheonix, AZ;
Donna J. and Lisa D., Seattle, WA.
And to Pam MacFetridge
for her editing,
and typesetting skills.

DROP THE ROCK

INTRODUCTION

S eems there was this group of 12 Step members taking a boat ride to this island called *Serenity*, and they were truly a happy bunch of people. As the boat pulled away from the dock, a few on board noticed Mary running down the street trying to catch up with the boat. One said, "Darn, she's missed the boat." Another said, "Maybe not. Come on, Mary! Jump in the water! Swim! Swim! You can make it! You can catch up with us!"

So Mary jumped into the water and started to swim for all she was worth. She swam for quite a while, and then started to sink. The members on board, now all aware that Mary was struggling, shouted, "Come on, Mary! Don't give up! Drop the rock!" With that encouragement, Mary started swimming again, only to start sinking again shortly afterward. She was going under when she heard all those voices shouting to her, "Mary, drop the rock! Let go, and drop the rock!"

Mary was vaguely aware of something around her neck, but she couldn't quite figure out what it was. Once more, she gathered her strength and started swimming. She was doing quite well, even gaining a little on the boat, but then she felt this heaviness pulling her under again. She saw all those people on the boat holding out their hands and hollering for her to keep swimming and shouting, "Don't be an idiot, Mary! Drop the rock!"

Then she understood, when she was going down for the third time. This thing around her neck, *this* was why she kept sinking when she really *wanted* to catch the boat. This thing was the "rock" they were all shouting about: resentments, fear, dishonesty, self-pity, intolerance and anger, just some of the things her "rock" was made of. "God help me get rid of the rock," she prayed. "Now! Get rid of it!"

So Mary managed to stay afloat long enough to untangle a few of the strings holding that rock around her neck, realizing as she did that her load was easing up; and then, with another burst of energy, *she let go.* She tore the other strings off and *dropped the rock.*

Once free of the rock, she was amazed how easy it was to swim, and she soon caught up with the boat. Those on board were cheering for her and applauding and telling her how great she was, and how it was so good having her with them again, and how now we can get on with our boat ride and have a nice time.

Mary felt great and was just about to indulge in a little rest and relaxation when she glanced back to shore. There, a ways back, she thought she saw something bobbing in the water, so she pointed it out to some others. Sure enough, someone was trying to catch the boat, swimming for dear life but not making much headway. In fact, it looked like they were going under.

Mary looked around and saw the concern on the faces of the other members. She was the first to lean over the rail and shout, "Hey, friend! Drop the Rock!"

◆ ◆ ◆

Mike shares his experience with dropping the rock:

Before its discussion of Step Four, the Big Book says: "Our liquor was but a symptom. So we had to get down to causes and conditions." A thorough inventory reveals those causes and conditions; the Fifth Step allows us to share them with God and another human being, and so remove the inner pain they have caused in our past lives.

After finishing my Fifth Step, I discarded the inventory but kept a single page that listed my major character defects. That list would come in handy later.

The first time I read Step Six, I thought it meant I had to arrive at some angelic state of mind in which I would become—and forever remain—"entirely ready" to have God remove all my defects. (I had forgotten that AA promises "spiritual progress rather than spiritual perfection.")

Twelve and Twelve set me right. It calls Step Six "AA's way of stating the best possible attitude one can take in order to make a beginning on this lifetime job." To me, that means Step Six is not a one-time matter; it stretches over a lifetime of recovery. Even that "best possible attitude" is always just a beginning.

A few years ago, while I was at Fellowship Club, I awoke very early one morning and knew it was time to make that beginning. I took out the list of defects, read it over, and asked myself two questions: "What are you holding on to these things for?" and "What did these things ever do *for* you?" (I may choose to hold on to them for fear of letting go, but holding on to them for years and years led me into alcoholism.) So I got on my knees and recited the Big Book's Step Seven prayer, which asks God's help in replacing our willfulness with His will for us. The *Twelve and Twelve* calls that replacement a "basic ingredient of all humility."

I arrived at Hazelden because I was sick and tired of being sick and tired. I believe we get active with Step Six when we get sick and tired of being sick—sick and tired of the character defects of which alcoholism is a symptom —sick and tired of their effect, not on our past, but on our present lives.

In this ongoing process, the Program is asking us to go where none of us has ever been before—into lives of lessened fear, diminished anger, fewer resentments, and genuine self-esteem instead of self-pity. There is a price, however: the willingness to **challenge and change** patterns of thought, speech, and behavior that may have gone unchallenged for ten, twenty, thirty years or more.

◆ ◆ ◆

These stories from Mary and Mike are good illustrations for a better understanding of working the Sixth and Seventh Steps. The first five Steps have supplied the foundation for recovery. The next two Steps begin the active day-to-day solution, removing what blocks us from *our usefulness* to other people, our Higher Power, and especially (and ultimately) from ourselves.

There are four basic reasons we won't be "entirely ready." First is a conscious decision that we will never give up a specific character defect. Next we blame our defects on others: people, situations, or institutions. Third, we rationalize. Our capacity to rationalize is unlimited. Before recovery we spent years on this one— throwing up barriers against unpleasant realities. Finally, the denial thing again: we are totally unaware of our own contribution to our problems.

The 12 Steps are written in order for a reason. There's not much use in doing our amends in Steps 8 and 9 if there is no sign of our willingness to change by doing Steps 6 and 7. How many times in active addiction did we say we were sorry without the slightest intent of changing our behavior so we wouldn't have to say we were sorry again? Working Steps 8 and 9 is hollow unless we've begun the active working of the Sixth Step with humility as our guide.

Let's look at the words of Sam Shoemaker to gain

some clarity on what the Sixth and Seventh Steps are asking of us. Sam was the Episcopal clergyman who ran Calvary Church and Mission where Bill W. (AA's co-founder and primary author of the Big Book) began his recovery. Bill W. credited Shoemaker with passing on to him and the early AAs the "spiritual keys" that make up the Program and the 12 Steps.

Shoemaker wrote about the necessity of making daily surrenders. Yes, the Sixth Step is also about surrendering, just like the Third. But Shoemaker made one point very clear: *We surrender as much of ourselves to as much of God as we understand*. In other words, our spiritual progress is based in direct proportion to our dropping the rock. We are very fortunate that all of our defects aren't revealed to us all at once. **The way the recovery process works is by gaining daily insight to what we can do in removing what blocks us.**

Shoemaker also passed on to the early AAs the idea that *God reveals as much truth as you can live up to*. That statement puts us directly on page 164 of the Big Book, where it says, "The answers will come, if your own house is in order." The Sixth Step helps us do that. Some have called the Sixth and Seventh Steps the "forgotten steps" because they aren't talked about that much. Others have called these Steps the most important.

By working the Sixth and Seventh Steps, we are less likely in recovery to stay stuck in old unproductive, negative behavior patterns. We gain more understanding on how all the Steps, although ordered for a reason, need also to be worked together. *This prevents us from falling into the trap of understanding only just enough of the Program to make us miserable and not enough to make us happy.*

The action of the Sixth and Seventh Steps culminates in dropping the rock—all the grasping and holding to old patterns of behavior, thinking, and feeling that are harmful to our progress in recovery.

For another insight, let's return to Shoemaker, who believed progress in the spiritual life is based on our *looking inward and upward, not outward and downward.*

Drop the Rock is a way of getting into the principals behind the Sixth and Seventh Steps, not only for understanding, but for action! We'll be looking at a number of ideas and examples of how men and women have made positive changes in their lives by working these Steps and showing up at meetings to tell others of their experiences.

After doing our Fifth Step, many of us were directed to go home and to read the paragraphs in the Big Book on the Sixth and Seventh Steps (a total of two paragraphs) then do the Steps. Who wouldn't want to be rid of those defects of character, especially after talking about them in the inventory process? All the pain and agony we dragged up, then told to another person and God, of course we wanted to be rid of those character flaws and habits. So, we prayed to let them go and humbly asked God for help. We thought we had done the Sixth and Seventh, and that was that.

Then, down the road, we started having the same difficulties and issues arising from defects that had plagued us before. We may not have practiced them or noticed them quite so much after doing a Fifth Step, but they returned with a force that scared and surprised us. We went back to our sponsor and said that perhaps we needed to do another Fourth and Fifth Step. We were feeling and acting very similar to ways we used to be. What should we do? Or, perhaps after years in the Program, things seemed to just have gone flat. There doesn't seem to be the same old spark and the meetings just aren't as interesting as they once were. We've drifted into a numb place, where there seems to be little growth and little reason to change.

Can we explain why we aren't entirely ready? Why can't we humbly ask? If not, what's in our way?

If our sponsor is a good one, perhaps he/she would respond that maybe it wasn't the Fourth or Fifth Step that needed repeating, but that it is time to take a real look at the Sixth and Seventh. Or, rather than blaming the Program and the people in it for the flatness in our life, it might be time to rejuvenate the growth process through a jump start of the Sixth and Seventh Steps, remembering the Program **helps those that help themselves.**

In this book, we, and all those who have assisted us, will attempt to take a real look at the Sixth and Seventh Steps. We must learn to take the intellectual knowledge and turn it into emotional and spiritual reality—into living—so we can continue to change and grow. To become the person we can become we must drop the rock—**all the grasping and holding on to old patterns of behaving, thinking, and feeling that are harmful to ourselves and to others.** The focus must become "moving toward completion" rather than "away from unpleasant and uncomfortable habits and actions."

Please join in this adventure of learning to put the Sixth and Seventh Steps into action. And through this action being able to transform our lives and relationships.

STEP SIX

Were entirely ready to have
God remove all these
defects of character.

A t the beginning of the discussion of the Sixth Step in the *Twelve and Twelve* it says, in a rather sexist way that this is the step that separates the men from the boys. Learning to be entirely ready—moving into total willingness—is very hard. It requires a great deal of work and a great deal of awareness.

Step Six requires us to stop struggling. It is time to acknowledge that we need help. Not only help to stop our addiction but help in living better lives. Having gone through Steps Four and Five, we are aware of our defects of character. Perhaps pride and thoughts of superiority are blocking the way to serenity. Or the habit of judging others. Perhaps it is a deep resentment, envy, or self-pity that keeps us in turmoil.

It is good to read Step Six over and over. It is brief and to the point. All it requires is becoming ready to become willing. We don't have to achieve change immediately. We can work on our attitude of mind, pray about it. We can think it over and see that our lives can become more trouble-free when we rid ourselves of destructive habits.

Relax. Step Six tells us. We don't do it all alone. Reflect. We turn to our Higher Power with confidence. Think of the relief that is waiting once we become entirely ready. It's like heading into a hot shower after working at a grubby chore. Feeling the dirt wash away is great. We emerge refreshed and shining and ready to deal with whatever comes our way.

We affirm to our Higher Power that we are ready to have God remove our defects and we continue in close and loving contact with God while we do our part in working on our shortcomings. Once we allow room for God to work in our lives we are making it possible for wonderful changes to take place. We all run into individuals in recovery who have given up the booze or other addiction: they are staying dry and/or abstinent only by *redirecting their intense inner misery into the lives of others.* They won't work the Sixth and Seventh Steps.

We'll be discussing the Sixth Step in terms of surrender. Surrender is mentioned many times in the Program, in many different contexts, yet it can be confusing and possibly misunderstood. For the Sixth Step, a spiritual surrender is necessary. Not a passive, waiting surrender, but an active use of the will, a total surrender of mind (thinking) and body (doing).

Surrender is usually brought up in the context of pain. When our life is unmanageable (and causing pain) we must "turn it over." When we decide to turn our life and our will over to the care of God "as we understand Him," we've opened the door to surrender. In the Third Step, it is the **decision** that is the key point—an active use of the will to turn it over, to align our will with God's. In the Sixth Step an even more active use of the will is required. We must act "as if" it has already taken place. We must have faith. Too many who take the Fifth Step make their confession and look around wondering where the solution lies.

Let's hear from Deb:

The Sixth Step is the perfectly logical place to be after having completed a thorough Fifth Step.

Asking ourselves. "Do I want to give this (defect) up?" is different than asking, "Do I want to be different?"

Regardless of what little I know about "being different," I must first ask, "Am I willing to believe that I *can* be different?" It is important to remember that Step Six doesn't say, "Became entirely ready to make myself different." It says, "Were entirely ready to have God remove these defects of character." God, not me makes me different by giving me what it takes to change. It is *my* job to act and behave like the change has occurred. In doing this, the process of change happens. Frequently this involves emotional pain; **the pain of living the way I have been becomes greater than the fear of change.** It also involves the pain of attracting seemingly obnoxious people. These folks are mirrors of my defects. I get to experience how it feels to have the shoe on the other foot.

This is a Step of surrender and trust, not *self-will* or self-determination. We surrender our ideas of which defects stand in the way of our usefulness to God.

Billy O. once gave me this example: "At a recovery convention someone I sponsor approached me to talk about a problem he was having. His mom was at the same convention and he was unable to "deal" with it. So he needed to talk to me about talking to her. I was practicing my defect of lust and enjoying being distracted by looking for available women. I blew him off. He ended up talking to his mom. I believe that God used my defect of lust to keep me unavailable to eliminate the middle man. The kid went straight to the source and used the tools he had to talk to his mom. This reminds me, how do I know when I'm being defective?"

God uses our defects and our assets in many ways to get His will accomplished.

Is there a "fast track" to spiritual perfection? or progress? It is important to get over and beyond the false pride of making "getting rid of character defects" a central focus of our lives. This approach is just one more way of not living life on life's terms. We get out into life and do the best we can with what we *know*. When we truly *know* better, we are willing to change. In the meantime, we live life.

The hardest aspect of Step Six is me not controlling it. It is me being *human* and *fallible*. Self-acceptance is more important that self-abuse. I cannot abuse myself into spirituality by shaming and ridiculing myself. I cannot open a flower with a sledgehammer—only God opens flowers. In Step Six, I must trust that Step Seven follows.

In the past many of us have approached Step Six with outrageous self-will to change, or in the other extreme, no will at all. I've found that there is no standard of reference for the amount of emotional pain that an individual needs or can endure before being motivated to change.

If I'm not changing my behavior because of pain, who am I trying to impress? Could it be that I'm trying to live up to an ideal in order to make an impression? To take control by redefining my self-image? Is this not still self-centeredness and self-will? Spiritual pride?

Yes, God uses defects to change me. But these questions are well worth asking ourselves as we consider our motives for change.

In Step Six our readiness to change comes from the awareness of how we are harming ourselves and there-fore God. It is gained in Step Five.

In order to remind myself that it is God's job, not mine, I use this prayer: "God, I don't care what I sound like, or look like, who my partners are, or where I live. I just don't want to be like this anymore. On Your terms, in Your time, *please* remake me as You will. Thank You."

I don't get to choose which defects God will remove, or

when I do get to live with it. I find that living with my defects continues to teach me humility. I find that the defects that made me an active threat to society were pretty much removed at once.

The defects that remove me from service are removed on and for the day that I ask. The rest of the defects, God lets me keep in order that I be reminded of my need for a daily spiritual contact. **They remind me that there is a God and it isn't me**.

In order to have God remove our character defects we must realize that we can't change ourselves by ourselves, or to any lasting good purpose without spiritual intervention. "Lack of power" is our dilemma. We find a Power by which we can live.

How do we know when we are entirely ready? How do we know when we're hungry? Some have experienced an entire readiness as a feeling of being completely burned out or being at the end of their rope. Other have received a sponsor's validation of readiness. Most of us experience this readiness after we have become very familiar with the feeling/experience of not being ready, or not being willing to be changed. We make friends with our defects and know how they have served us. This results in knowing how they no longer serve us.

Defects of character are our best attempts to get our needs met. They have saved our lives. My problem was one of ignorance; I didn't know what my basic human needs were and therefore didn't know how to meet them. This is where "as you learn better you do better" applies. The hole in me, the neediness, the hunger, the ache in my life that I tried to fill/or stay distracted from by using addictive behavior is actually the perfectly logical result of not knowing and therefore not accepting myself as I am.

I was wrong, not bad. I did "look bad." And I didn't get my needs met, so I ignorantly, apparently insanely, and desperately repeated what I knew. More, more, and more; or less, less, and less. Deprivation and over-consumption are flip sides of the same coin. ***The point of recovery is finding the balance.***

◆ ◆ ◆

Finding balance incorporates the awareness gained in Steps Four and Five with the action (the behavior changes and prayer) gained in Steps Six and Seven. Like the pendulum, we do swing from one extreme of behavior to another, yet those points of extreme slowly become less far apart. We change.

Like in the First Step, finding balance involves *admitting* (accepting as true and valid to our selves) that past attempts to meet our needs have failed. It is recognizing that we are truly bodily and mentally differ-ent than our fellows. That a predictable aspect of our disease is extreme action: consumption, deprivation, or repetition. This is how we become ready for finding the balance. We get to experience it. Yes, we do supply the willingness, but it is God who supplies the changes, and the reasons for our willingness.

Wanting to become willing to feel different is not foreign to us. It was this willingness that we used to feed our addictive behaviors. We wanted to feel different. Now, though, we ask God, and we become ready to have character defects removed by using our awareness of ourselves and our will to be different.

In surrendering, we are saying our way hasn't worked (what a surprise!). We are willing to try it another way. We desire to be at peace with our beliefs. We are fortunate people. We have the opportunity to face the battle of understanding our lives. We have another go-round at a life once abandoned. We want to be winners, securely and absolutely. The willingness can be a sane and healthy choice or a reactive choice because of pain. We all get to choose—sooner or later, we get to choose. In looking at working the Sixth Step, it is this approach that separates the winners from the losers. **The winners actively seek and practice a new way of living. A new way of being. A new way of thinking. A new way of behaving. A new way of relating.** The losers wait until they are in so much pain that the choice becomes obvious, and then they choose to participate in only enough to get the pain to stop.

Karen shares a realization she has had:

Recently, I was perusing ahead in my daily mediation book when I came upon a quote by Martha Roth which piqued my curiosity. "Insight is cheap," she said. My first reaction was "Gee, I don't agree with her. We in recovery place high value on insight. After all, it's our insight regarding the problem of addiction which makes us particularly helpful to 'the person who still suffers,'" but, as I read the short essay following the quote, I began to see Ms. Roth's point.

She talked about people who *analyze* themselves to death. They know exactly what makes them do the things they do: the tyrannical mothers, the abusive husbands, the poverty they were raised in or the childhood of extreme indulgence, ad nauseam.

They have great insight; but instead of using that insight as a means to develop new and, hopefully, better behavior, they use it as a reason to continue with old, destructive behavior. They are not willing to go through the pain it takes to change, even though the pain of staying the same is killing them.

They are victims. The list of people who've done them wrong is long, and the list of those people whose expectations they cannot live up to is even longer. They cling to their character defects with alarming tenacity, all the while blaming everything and everyone for their problems.

In fact, they don't see their poor behavior as character

defects at all, but more like genetic anomalies, such as bowlegs or thin hair, or the permanent result of improper socialization by parents who in most cases did the best job they could.

Admitting that they might be somewhat at fault, they are sure others are more to blame. Therefore, instead of asking God to remove any defects of character, they secretly curse God for dealing them such a lousy hand.

They are good at working with newcomers, especially if the newcomer is attractive and a member of the opposite sex (or same sex, if they are so inclined). The problem here is that all they want to do is talk about themselves and all the newcomer wants to do is talk about themselves, so these liaisons rarely last more than a few days or weeks before they bore each other to the brink of suicide.

While they rarely balk at Steps 4 and 5 because those Steps give them the opportunity once again to dwell on their most beloved topic, themselves, they seem to get stuck at this point and gloss over or ignore completely those Steps in the Program which are vital to emotional and spiritual recovery: Steps 6 and 7.

And, without emotional and spiritual recovery, you don't have much. You have abstinence, and you may not even have that for very long.

◆ ◆ ◆

Choosing to move into willingness and being willing to choose (e.g. take responsibility) is a positive way of living. It is saying about myself "Hey, I'm worth moving toward being different without pain. I value myself and others enough to choose to make changes now, rather than wait until I can't stand not making a choice." It is a completely different perspective than waiting until it hurts to make choices. The majority of us are very aware of defects of character, but often it isn't until we are "sick and tired of being sick and tired" that we become willing to change.

Acting "as if" the choice is already made and the changes in our lives are already in place puts the power of our will in line with the power of the universe so that we move forward more gracefully into living without defects.

Will it work? About as well as we surrender. Will it change our lives? Yes, without question.

It is a matter of practicing and willingness; using the Steps we've already taken to maintain our commitment. The more willing we become, and the more we practice acting "as if," the more active our surrender becomes and the more we are able to live "as if." It is a very fulfilling and rewarding process. Acting "as if" can raise questions of genuineness and authenticity. Is there a conflict with who I am choosing to become and who I currently am? What if I act as if the changes have already taken place?

Authenticity is being true to a vision and purpose. We are authentic when we choose to act and feel and choose to behave in balance with the higher values and principles we've chosen for our lives. If those principles and values are not fully in place and manifested, it doesn't make us phony. *It makes us human.* If we feel the conflict between who we are and who we would become, it is good. It signals that we understand the difference between reality and fantasy, and are moving toward reality.

There are many stages in surrendering and practicing. It's called **progress**. We will be discussing many of the stages in connection with the Sixth Step and again in working with the Seventh. We will be discussing many of the things which hinder our ability to surrender and many of the very defects of character that we may wish to remove. There is no magic in recovery. We get what we work for.

Let's take a look at Charlie's story:

When I first came in, I wanted all the good things people had but I didn't want to work for them. Oh, I worked the Steps—at least the ones I thought I needed. And when it came to Steps 6 and 7, I was ready and willing to have my Higher Power remove my shortcomings—should I have any, of course. I had no idea what they were because I didn't think I needed Steps 4 and 5. But I prayed, vaguely, that should He see any shortcomings, I was ready for Him to remove them. The principle of Step 7 is humility. I had none.

As I made progress in recovery, I became aware of many character defects and of just how blind I had been to them. Mercifully, my Higher Power showed me only what I was ready to see.

I became depressed and thought I could never be forgiven for or relieved from these shortcomings. This depression, I discovered, was not humility, but another form of "playing God," **believing my character defects were more powerful than my Higher Power's forgiveness.**

Then, when I recognized Who had the power and who was powerless, I had to decide if I was "entirely ready" to ask Him to remove my shortcomings. After all, my character defects were what I thought made up my personality, and I was pretty much in love with who I thought I was. Self-will had been my HP for a lifetime. I was afraid, not knowing that something better would take the place of my character defects.

With all the honesty I was capable of at the time, I worked the Steps in order, 1 through 6, then 7, asking as humbly as I could that my Higher Power remove my shortcomings. They did not disappear. I was not struck pure.

Then I was made aware that character defects are like active addiction. I couldn't keep using and expect

God to relieve my disease. ***Neither could I keep
practicing my character defects and expect God to
remove them.***

I was going to have to develop a new set of habits—
to work against who I thought I'd always been—and as
I practiced these new habits, the old habits/character
defects would begin to be replaced. This creates a period
of grieving which doesn't make sense at first. Why
should I hurt over the leaving (letting go/having removed) of behaviors that only harmed me?

And so I began really living the Program, the daily
striving to change, to let go and receive more. It didn't
happen overnight. It took years of practice. I am not a
saint. But I claim, accept, and am grateful for my
spiritual progress.

◆ ◆ ◆

Charlie made some very important discoveries in his
journey. In the context of surrender that we are discussing here, the first thing he discovered was that he needed
to be willing to make a choice. It was up to Charlie to put
his will into action and to choose to work the Steps and
to practice being willing until he was entirely willing.
The next thing he discovered was that his own resistance
to surrendering was because his self-concept was that
his personality was his character defects. If he gave up
his shortcomings, he'd become the "hole in the donut."
Which is the essence of faith—***it is trusting that God
will reshape me into what I was meant to be in the
first place.***

How many times have you heard that at meetings?
Probably many, many times. We fear becoming invisible
if we stop practicing our faults. Moreover, we fear
becoming average, normal, or boring. In contemplating
surrender, many of us come face to face with our self-
image in an honest fashion for the first time. We may

have glimpsed it in Step 5, which can be a very difficult realization. We've spent a lifetime building an image of who we are and how we operate, then we are asked to put it aside when it is in conflict with the new principles we've decided to follow in the Program. No wonder we have fear and misgivings.

Here is where we must contemplate the nature of our true, authentic selves and who we would become, our willingness to go to any length for recovery. It is an act of will—a choice—and we must be willing to assume accountability for that choice. *Steps 6 and 7 do not say who we would become, but who we don't want to be.* It is very threatening to the ideas we've held about ourselves when we must choose who we would become. Our defects, many times, are our best friends. If I become (choose to be) "entirely ready" and my character defects lessen or disappear, who will I be?

As it talks about in the *Twelve and Twelve*, it is not the blatantly obvious character defects that we have problems giving up, it is the ones we practice "in moderation" or only on occasion that are the most difficult. What appear to be natural drives seem to become our enemies when we start to contemplate and prepare to work Step Six. In becoming entirely ready—in deciding to be willing to surrender—that we must examine our hearts and work with prayer and contemplation to set aside self-image and move into self-awareness.

Let's take a look at Pat's story:

When I was about three years in recovery, I had a real crisis of faith. I didn't feel I was moving and changing enough in the Program and I wasn't confident that the people who were saying not to worry about becoming the "hole in the donut" had enough of what I wanted to be trustworthy. I went outside the Program for help through therapy and came face to face with a counselor who told me I needed to work a Third Step. That was the last thing I wanted to hear.

He also got me thinking about Steps Six and Seven. I was very afraid of losing those things that made me *me*. Would I give up my intensity and aggressiveness? Would I lose my edge? Would I become "spiritual" and monk-like? How would I handle life without some of my more important pieces? It caused me a great deal of discomfort and, occasionally, some outright fear.

In working through some of these issues with my sponsor and talking about them in meetings, I began to realize that the things that make me who I am are not defined by my actions. *I wasn't just attending meetings anymore to avoid doing what I needed doing outside of meetings.* All the defects that I have become glaringly obvious through my actions...but that does not define me as a person. I may act badly on occasion. That doesn't make me a bad person.

So, I started looking at giving up and releasing those parts of me—those habits of action—that were defective and self-defeating. Finally I was working on the Steps *outside* meetings instead of just talking about them *at* meetings. I saw my character defects as glitches to be corrected rather than major portions of my framework. Sometimes it felt pretty major. But, as I learned to surrender and release, how I defined myself began to change, too. Now, I seek the opportunity to look at defects and let them go. Something new and better always seems available to take its place. Over the years in recovery, I have slowly developed a deep belief that I can solve the problem and find the willingness to do so.

◆ ◆ ◆

It becomes apparent in Pat's story and many like it that the "hole in the donut" fear is a shadow boxer. It can cause us alarm, but if we do the work and move forward, it gradually disappears in the light. **It disappears in proportion to our understanding of who our Higher Power is and how the God of our understanding works in our lives.** Pat also brought up a point about trust. We will look very closely at trust when we get into the Seventh Step. For now it is enough to say that trust is an ongoing issue with almost everyone in recovery.

We'll take a look now at ways of taking action and those things that cause us to resist taking action in moving into becoming *entirely ready*.

ACTION

For many of us, working the Steps has meant going to meetings and talking about the Steps and what they've meant in our lives. Or working the Steps so we can talk about them in meetings. Occasionally, we've been forced into taking action, like doing a Fourth Step inventory or talking out a Fifth Step. Making amends calls for action. Usually, however, after taking those specific actions, we're done with it. Steps Six and Seven, in particular, become "nodders." We go to meetings where Six and Seven are discussed and nod wisely and serenely with almost every comment that is made. When it is our turn to talk we explain about getting into the Sixth and Seventh after doing our inventory and taking a Fifth Step. And, we all feel like we're working the Steps.

It is a challenge to take another look at that process. Talking about the Steps at meetings is much different than working them. Remember Chapter 6 in the Big Book, where these Steps are outlined, is called "Into Action." Having done a little work or action on a Step in the past is a far cry from continuing to work it now. Nodding at meetings in agreement with a particularly profound comment is not the same as doing what the speaker may have done to reach that awareness.

We must become willing to take action—continuous

action—to become who we can become. It takes awareness to become entirely ready. Slow down, stop doing and
be. Feel it.

Here's Richard's perspective on Step 6:

I had enjoyed many rewards from the Program,
experienced many of the feelings of liberation my
sponsor had promised, and still after two years of working the Steps something was missing. There remained
lingering feelings of discontent. The personality flaws I
had uncovered in doing the Fourth and Fifth had diminished but were still there. And they produced thoughts
and feelings I had while using—impatience, intolerance,
quick temper, arrogance, and especially an unforgiving
attitude toward others and myself.

So I had lunch with my sponsor and discussed my
situation with him. After talking a while and asking
many questions, he asked, "You really think you've done
all the Steps, don't you?" I assured him, somewhat
indignantly, that I had. Hadn't I done the Fourth and
Fifth with him? Had not he seen my Twelfth Step
actively with his own eyes? Wasn't he aware of how
faithfully—in my mind—I was doing the Tenth and
Eleventh Steps?

"All very true," he said, "but what about the *Sixth*
Step?" He went on by telling me a story. It seemed one
night there was a man down on his hands and knees
looking frantically for something on the sidewalk under
a street lamp. A policeman stopped by and asked him
what he was doing? "I've lost my keys," answered the
man. "Will you help me look for them?" The policeman
joined in and after a while asked, "Are you sure you
dropped them here?" The man looked up and said, "No.
I dropped them back there—but there it is much too
dark." The policeman asked, "Why are we looking here
then?" With all sincerity he answered, "Because here is

where the light is, and I'm afraid of the dark." Finished with the story, my sponsor again asked, "What about the *Sixth* Step?"

I was shocked he could ask me such a question. Of course, I was willing to change and have my Higher Power remove my defects of character, wasn't I—*Was I?*

If I was sincerely willing to change, why did I remain so much the same? I realized that perhaps I had been paying lip service to the Sixth Step. Compared to most of the other Steps, the Sixth appeared simple. I believed this, because no overt action seemed required. There is none of the dramatic confrontation that exists when we do the Ninth Step, nor is there the feeling of accomplishment that comes with the Twelfth. The Sixth is not dramatic. There are no enthusiastic witnesses to rush up and shake one's hand. It's a rather solitary affair and hence seems simple.

The Sixth Step means facing ourselves, and that is usually more difficult than being honest with another person. I have found it difficult to lie to others because of practicing the principles of the Program, but still easily lie to myself. When I say, all too swiftly, "Of course I'm willing to change," I know I will ask myself, "Really? Who's kidding who?" *The fact that I will daily question my willingness to change, will increase my ability to be increasingly willing.* I simply won't take the process as lightly as I have before. I can't learn anything unless I'm sincerely willing to learn. Nor will making myself promises to change have any significance until the willingness factor is developed.

My sponsor intervened again with a few of his pointed questions. "You played football in school, didn't you?" he asked—knowing full well I had. He reminded me that I told him I hated the practice, "getting those bumps and bruises for no good reason." And he also reminded me how I had said I loved the actual game, especially the cheers when I did something very well.

"You know," he said, "no one gets all excited about practice. It has no flash to it. It's the game that counts. But a good game performance requires hard practice. And the Sixth Step can be compared with football practice. If you're going to make continuing progress in the Program, you really have to work the Sixth and Seventh Step. You can't stand around on one foot waiting for applause. There won't be any if you don't keep practicing."

What my sponsor told me that day still carries an important moral lesson. It's one I'm continually diligently learning, because I now—finally—am seeing the true value in the Sixth Step. Like the man looking for his keys in the wrong place, I too was looking in the wrong place to become *entirely ready* in the Sixth Step. I'm making progress in facing my fears and venturing *into the dark of my unwillingness* to have my character defects removed.

I am continually repeating the rather paradoxical sentence I came up with that helps me with the way I now look at the Sixth Step, ***the fact that I will daily question my willingness to change, will increase my ability to be increasingly willing.***

◆ ◆ ◆

It is important to discuss another aspect of recovery at this point in order to gain a different perspective than what we may have held about the Program in the past. If we think that recovery is strictly about abstinence from alcohol (drugs, food, sex, gambling, etc.) and that staying abstinent will solve all the major problems in life, then we probably won't want to hear what comes next. If, on the other hand, we feel that recovery is about living fully and freely and about reaching toward our potential, then we might be interested in this.

A friend of ours, who is not in recovery, mentioned to

us an observation he had made about folks in recovery. He felt that recovering people spent almost all their time learning to stand up and helping others stand up, but very few spent any time walking. If "walking" in this analogy means getting on with a meaningful and purposeful life, there is some truth in his observation. We get so caught up in our own abstinence, or going to meetings and helping others recover that we lose sight of the "larger picture." Sure, there is great meaning in helping others recover. And, helping others is a great way to move into humility (which we discuss in depth in Step Seven) and to gain a spiritual perspective on life. Helping others to stand, however, is not quite as meaningful as helping others learn to walk. Nor is it as meaningful as helping others find a direction and destination to walk towards. ***We help others by setting the example rather than telling them the example.*** We learn to shift our vision to the horizon, rather than watching our feet. This is extremely important when we are looking to continue to grow and let go of those things that may limit our ability to do so.

So, the first act is to become **aware**, second is **acceptance**, then third is to **surrender**. Once we have chosen to be willing to surrender, we move on to those things that can help our surrendering and our awareness of what it is we're giving up. The choice to surrender, the becoming entirely ready, is just that—a choice. Awareness, however, is an entirely different matter.

To make surrender effective, we must be willing to help the process by using our awareness to move into line with the surrender. We must choose to "act as if." And our awareness must shift so we become aware *when* we aren't acting in accordance with that choice. Changing our awareness can be a slow process or it can be instantaneous. With grace, it can happen smoothly and quickly. When we are struggling, it can seem to take forever. The difference is willingness. When we stay honest, willing, and especially open-minded, we stay aware.

Lisa adds how "acting as if" helped her with the Sixth Step:
My sponsor gave me a typed piece of paper and told me to put it on my bathroom mirror and read it daily. *In the arena of human life the honors and rewards fall to those who show their good qualities in action.* I did as my sponsor suggested and with that sentence staring at me all the time has helped me with my continuing readiness. The good character qualities I want to have are only demonstrated to me and others by my actions.

But the only way for me to get there, to get what I needed was to "act as if" I had it. The key word is "act." I have discovered in my case that knowledge often follows action rather than vice versa. When I *faked* it in my early days, I found myself *making* it in later days.

In the beginning, I was asked to "act as if" I was following instructions, trusting the Program, listening to my sponsor, and coming to believe. The amazing thing was soon I was doing those very things.

I was never able to think my way into recovery. My mind created a tremendous amount of trouble for me. I needed to turn my mind down (not off). I soon discovered the difference between doing and thinking. The key to "acting as if" is faith. The way to faith is *through* my fears. I have made progress and stay *entirely ready* when I turn fears over to my faith and simply "act as if."

◆ ◆ ◆

As we discussed, acting "as if" can seem to be in conflict with being genuine and authentic. However, when we are willing (making choices) to make positive progress and to have God shape us toward our potential as spiritual beings, then acting in accordance with those intentions is very genuine in spite of our best intentions.

One of the things we must be careful of is our capacity for drama.

It seems as if addiction is a path toward drama. Perhaps because most of us repressed and suppressed feelings from the very beginning, we learned to be dramatic when it was important for our feelings to be noticed. We also learned to be dramatic to hide our true feelings—even from ourselves. Even though it is important to validate, feel and identify our feelings, we must be careful not to dramatize. When we are moving toward becoming "entirely ready" it is easy to be self-absorbed and dramatic about our path. We must be willing to quietly move toward *self-examination, rather than self-absorption*. As we practice, this difference becomes more evident.

Here are some of the things we can do to make this process move more quickly and easily:

1) We can develop or borrow a ritual to mark our surrender and choice to become ready. The power of ritual is incredible and we can use that power to help move into balance with our choice. Think about a candle ceremony, perhaps burning up slips of paper with your hesitations and fears and character defects written out on them. Or walk on the beach and write out in the sand at the water's edge all the things that concern and trouble you about surrendering, then watch the waves erase the words and your cares. Perhaps put your thoughts and fears and feelings on slips of papers in bottles and set them sailing into the sunset at the ocean.

Or ask your sponsor. Or ask at meetings. Read about rituals and borrow one that feels good and significant to you or make up a simple, powerful ritual marking your decision to become "entirely ready."

Rituals are rites of passage, as is the Sixth Step. Using a ritual for this powerful method of transformation personalizes the experience.

Let's hear from Betty:

I have attacked Step Six many times. It has attacked me in return. We have had open warfare, and we have had peace. For periods of time, I have on purpose ignored this Step. I have said that it made no sense to me.

The battle began some years back, when I regularly attended Step-discussion meetings. I had done my best on the first Five Steps, I thought. I had even made a written list of all my defects. They counted up to thirty.

Following the example of an old-timer friend of mine, whose quality of recovery I admired, I printed, in ink, each of my separate defects on a poker chip. Then all thirty chips went into a small pitcher. Every morning on awaking, I plunged my hand into it (like picking a number from a goldfish bowl) and came up with the "chip for today." The defect might be anger, fear, pride, resentment, gossip, arrogance, self-pity, procrastination, anxiety, intolerance, and so on, but whichever one it was had to be concentrated on for the next 24 hours, and either reduced to a minimum or cast away.

It was a kind of game. I enjoyed wrestling with one "defect" a day. I felt I was making progress, really working the Program. It hadn't occurred to me that I had gone overboard on this "defect" business. Thirty indeed! How is it that for the "pride" defect? Of course, most of them were not serious flaws of character such as the inability to be honest with oneself. Most were bad habits possessed, in some degree, by most humans.

Nevertheless, I kept up this game for two or three years, telling many fellow members about it and urging them to go and do likewise. I explained that, although the Step suggested that God would remove these defects when and if I became ready to let go of them, I was of the school that believed in the saying "Pray for potatoes, but pick up the hoe." I did ask my Higher Power to lend a hand on the defect I happened to confront each day, but

I felt that God expected me to use energy on rooting it out of my character all by myself.

Still those dozens of defects I had laid claim to kept cropping up again and again, over and over. It seemed that the harder I fought them, the harder they fought back. I became very discouraged. I decided I had been willing, I had tried, and I would now let Number Six, and myself, have a vacation. I put the little pitcher with its chips on the shelf, behind some books and only now and then dipped into it. I kept busy and active in the Program; I felt comfortable in recovery; I was trying to practice the principles in all my affairs. Then, out of nowhere, came a deep resentment toward a fellow member. I agonized over it, prayed over it, but discussed it with no one. I had insomnia, indigestion, and fatigue. (Any good doctor can tell you that negative emotions make people physically ill.)

Fortunately, just about that time our group was slated for discussion of Step Six. I opened my copy of the *Twelve and Twelve* and read the Step all the way through. Although I had read it many times before, it seemed as if I saw its meaning for the first time. I gathered that, instead of fighting mightily against a defect, I also had to let go of it. Just simply open up my hands, my heart, and my mind and say to my Higher Power, "Here it is, this defect. I give it to You. Please remove it from me." In this case, it was the bitter and destructive resentment that I wished to be rid of. And so it happened. It faded away and never returned.

Since then, I have followed the same procedure on other emotional problems, with the same result. I just have to keep in mind that if I am not 100 percent sincere in my *willingness* to be rid of the problem, the procedure won't work. I have come to realize that Step Six means exactly what it says. No more, no less. When, and if, I become ready to have painful, inhibiting, or long-stand-

ing flaws removed, they will be. Not always perma-
nently, not all of them. But if and when they return, they
will be weaker and much easier to let go of. As for all
those bad habits I once listed as defects, I am trying to
arrest them one day at a time, as I do my addiction.

A little progress has been made on pride. I can now
admit that most of my troubles stem from one large and
glaring defect: **self-centeredness**. For how can I
wallow in self-pity, weep over resentments, be sick with
righteous anger, ache with envy, and tense up with fears
and anxieties unless all my thoughts are exclusively on
poor me?

A long time ago, a very wise person wrote: "A person's
life is what their thoughts make it." Through Step Six,
I have learned how true that is. I may never comprehend
fully, yet I know its value to me. It calls forth the most
precious asset any recovering person can have: the
willingness to get out of the driver's seat, to stop trying
to run the show. I need to keep the Sixth Step and
Seventh Step message of letting go and letting God in my
thoughts at all times.

◆ ◆ ◆

2) Use prayer. Your ritual can include prayer. Your
daily meditation and practice can include prayer. We'll
talk about prayer in connection with the Seventh Step,
also, but it is essential in the Sixth. As in all the Steps,
prayer as a part of ritual is doubly potent and can add
depth and meaning to any commitment you decide to
make (e.g. willingness to be or stay willing).

Use prayer to ask for awareness and willingness to
receive. Use prayer to ask for depth and clarity. Use
prayer to ask to become a better conduit of your Higher
Power. Use prayer to ask for ease and grace in surrender.
Use prayer to ask how to pray. Use prayer to ask how to
think and act. Use prayer to say "thank you." Use

prayer. Prayer can be considered **cheating** because of how much easier it makes the process go.

Prayer is of no use when it is not used. Prayer is not only a matter of belief. It is a matter of practice. We can't get caught in the trap of dogma or method. Prayer is not about right or wrong or "should" or "only." It is about a personal or individualized way to talk with God or your Higher Power or Universal Energy or the collective unconscious or whatever you want to call it. Prayer is not about someone else telling us how to pray or what to say. *It is about communication.*

There are some extremely effective prayers from many spiritual traditions. These prayers became effective because the people who wrote them or said them practiced them daily. The saints who used prayer were not worried about doing it right. They were concerned with communing with God and gaining clarity for their own action. We continually need to take a closer look at prayer and its place in our life. It can be very revealing.

Many members become boosters of prayer only after having resisted using it. It just didn't seem necessary to them or even admirable. People who needed and used prayer seemed to be a rung lower on the ladder than those who could get things done. Self-will vs. God's will.

It was only after getting involved in prayer through a spiritual search and surrender, then practicing it, that we come to understand its depth and meaning. Prayer is not something to be intellectualized and analyzed. It can only be realized through practice. The Program urges us to take action. Pray. An often quoted prayer goes like this, "God give me the courage and strength to know who I really am, to act accordingly in my life, and to refrain from diverting my time, energy, and interest into my character defects."

3) Learn to meditate. Meditation and prayer are traditionally discussed in the Eleventh Step, but you can put them to use here, if you choose. Those in the Program for a while realize that the steps are synergistic, and that after a while they will be practicing parts of one with many others, all at the same time. Meditation is a practice that can be utilized throughout the whole Program. Meditation is mostly about listening.

Although not much is said in the Big Book or the *Twelve and Twelve* about how to meditate, we are instructed to practice and become intuitive to the presence of God. We practice meditation as a discipline in our own way until we have made it a regular part of our routine. Some members benefit by reading books which are available about meditation and its methods. Others have attended classes at their local community college, yoga center, or church. Like prayer and other positive disciplines in recovery, the benefits of meditation only become apparent through practice.

In using meditation for the Sixth Step, a form of contemplation can be used. Taking a single word or thought and letting it run through our mind can be very revealing. Take for example the word "surrender." We may start repeating the word in our mind like: "Surrender. Surrender. Surrender. Give up. Release. Let go. Surrender. Peace. Renewal. Surrender. Vulnerable. Open. Surrender. Surrender. Strength. Change. Higher Power. Surrender." We can keep this type of string of thoughts going for a while, probably no more than five minutes to start, as we do our regular morning or evening routine of prayer and meditation.

Prayer is seeking answers and direction in life. Meditation is listening for answers from a Higher Power and developing the ability within ourselves to accept the answers. Reflection is the study of ways to turn the answers we get from prayer and meditation into action.

Reflection is the study of the meaning and uses of the Twelve Steps. It is not snap judgment. It requires consideration of the pros and cons of our possible choices and determination of what directions we will take to give us the best results. *The progress of spirituality from prayer to meditation to reflection is active, not passive.* It is taking part in the joy of putting the results of prayer and meditation into action. We learn through times of quiet reflection to work into our lives the answers our Higher Power has given us as a result of our prayer and meditation.

Prayer, meditation, and reflection will also give us greater awareness of our particular forms of resistance. This knowledge lets us know how we are doing it wrong—like finding out our shoelaces aren't tied together—so we can tie them. In this type of contemplation a new awareness and focus will arise. If we are uncomfortable with meditation and prayer, we try learning some simple practices of quieting the mind and gaining concentration. We use our intuition and sense of higher purpose to find a comfortable method to practice becoming "entirely ready." We gain clarity and vision. Meditation will help in determining the shape of our prayer and the direction of our surrender.

4) The next course of action is that of cleansing. If we are to engage in a new course of action and become "entirely ready" to get rid of our defects, it makes sense that we start from a clean slate. Of course, common sense is a very rare thing in or out of the Program. So, it is not surprising that it is rarely discussed in meetings that we might need to make an effort to get to a clean place where we can start.

Let's take a look at a few areas that we may want to examine and clean up as we prepare to become entirely ready.

How is our language used? Are we gaining maturity? Do we swear a lot and make crude remarks about the opposite sex and use biased and prejudiced language? Do we tell dirty or risqué jokes? Do we use violent language? We take a look at our language and see how it fits in with a spiritual approach to living and to becoming entirely ready.

Many are amazed at the amount of swearing at meetings when they first start attending. Smoking, swearing, making fun of those less fortunate seemed to be an accepted thing. It was like the jokes survivors tell to overcome their fear and to show the relief that is felt. We need to examine this very closely. How does a person who has taken a Third Step and is practicing and preparing a Step Six and Seven talk? Try giving up swearing. Try giving up violent language. Try giving up bias. Try giving up sexism. We become willing to give them up and act "as if" until God removes them.

Another area to look at closely is all other addictive practices. Language patterns can be addictive. Do you still smoke, binge on sugar, excessively drink coffee, recklessly gamble, abuse credit cards, act out sexually, drive over the speed limit . . .? How does that affect your movement toward God and spirituality? Does practicing one addiction mean that we still have an addictive lifestyle? Remember what it says in the Big Book about alcohol (drugs, food, sex, gambling, etc.) being a symptom. It is just the tip of the iceberg. We need to examine closely our whole lives for addictive and abusive patterns. If we are to give up our defects of character, we need to become willing to see them all!

We examine our sexual life and how we relate to the opposite sex. (Or the same sex, if that is our preference.) Do we use sex to mood alter? Are we abusive? Are we able to be intimate? Can we reveal our true feelings in an open and trusting manner? Can we relate well with the opposite sex without becoming sexual? What is the pattern in our relationships?

Are we addicted to caffeine? Or gum? Or any substance? (Very interesting phenomenon when we start to judge those things we deem to be less threatening to our sobriety, and therefore okay to keep. We really start to rationalize and explain. The fact is that it is addictive. Period. We can't afford to kid ourselves about that any more than we can about smoking or drinking or gambling or sexing or any other addictions. Addictions all mask feelings and change the way we deal with ourselves and others. We need to deal with them all.)

How about our work patterns? Are we a workaholic? Do we avoid our family and other issues by working tremendously long hours? Do we rationalize the time spent away from home with the explanation that we need to work this hard to keep our job? Economically times are hard, so we need to put in the extra effort in order to remain secure? Do we gain the major satisfaction and meaning from life through our work? Are we willing to look at how we work? Are we completely identified by the results of our work? Work is an area that many of us are afraid of looking at. We might find that we use work to mood alter. We might find that we use work to avoid. We might find that work is much more than a job. It is very much worth examining.

How about exercise? Do we use exercise to mood alter? Do you become addicted to exercise and the results of exercise? Do you avoid through exercise? Like work, this is a tough one to examine. We all need to exercise, so how much is too much? That is why we are taking a close look now. With prayer and meditation, we hope to find a balance point that is in line with our spiritual intent and our ability to share.

So, let's look at cleansing to move toward becoming ready.

The first cleansing action suggested is to examine what we eat and drink. Pick a day. Use the day to examine our eating habits and drinking habits. Look at how you eat food and your rituals of eating.

The second cleansing action we suggest is to make a special retreat, maybe for a weekend, at least for a day, to practice our examinations and cleansing rituals and to look at becoming entirely ready. Maybe we can go to the mountains or the beach. Maybe a friend has a cabin or summer home we can borrow. It should be a place away from our normal routine, where we can be quiet and contemplative. Use the retreat to become as open as possible to all the actions necessary to becoming entirely ready.

Another cleansing action many find helpful is to make a day of silence. Don't speak for twenty four hours. Don't listen to the radio or stereo. Don't watch TV. Don't distract yourself with any diversions. Just be quiet and open. Let the world enter you quietly. Contemplate this quote by Publius: "I have often regretted my speech, never my silence."

The next cleansing action suggested is a period of celibacy. We take some time—a week or more—to examine our sexual patterns and relationship patterns. We learn to become open to relating in a non-sexual manner. We take a close look at our own sexuality and how comfortable we are with it. Be open to our intuition and our spirituality in our sexual life.

The last cleansing action suggested is to release the clutter in our life. We take a look in our storage areas and garage. Getting rid of the stuff we've been packing around for years every time we move. Giving it to a charitable organization. We take a look in our closets...possibly, if we haven't worn it in a year or a year and a half, we give it away. **The point is, we quit holding on to things that are useless to us.** They may be very important to someone else who will use or wear them. We clean up our house or apartment. Those things we don't use, but have been holding on to "just in case" are let go. Release them. This way we make room in our life for new and exciting things. This is more than just a physical act. **It is symbolic of opening our life, mentally, emotionally, spiritually for new things.** It is very hard to reach for new adventures and growth in our lives when our hands are full, holding on to the baggage and excesses of our past. We are grateful for what we have in our life. Taking nothing for granted. Releasing what we can. *Getting ready to become more, and less, and better.*

Judith shares a story of her attempts to deal with clutter:

The first time my sponsor visited my house, she was taken aback by how messy my apartment was. She went on and on about the importance of keeping my place clean and how a messy place had a dramatic effect, possibly more on an unconscious level, on my general outlook on my life and recovery.

I told her I just couldn't seem to keep my house in order which resulted in living in a mess all the time. I related feebly that I had turned the problem over to my Higher Power and I had been praying to have God clean my house. Of course I had been mistaken then about the role of my Higher Power in my recovery. Then I went through the "being stuck on the Third Step" phase, where if my house is messy, it must be God's will that I live in a mess.

My sponsor and I had a good laugh about my first two attempts to deal with my messy house and how these ideas typically visit most of us in recovery as we make progress in understanding how the Steps work in our lives. I now know that if I don't want to live in a mess, I need to pray to God for the willingness, courage, and motivation to clean up my own house.

If we can think of any other areas in our life that we'd like to be able to have a clearer understanding of, design a cleansing exercise to gain a new perspective. There is no better time than *now* to look at all the troubled areas in our life. We are getting ready to make over all those areas, so we become willing to examine them.

Here is an example from Pam:

Five years into recovery, I noticed that my spiritual life— my life in general—seemed empty and less than it could be. My marriage was not in trouble, but it was not a vibrant, joyful joining together of two people in love. My job was a job—full of stress, lots of demands, little satisfaction, and I seemed to be spending more and more time doing it. I had friends and activities, but had little time to give to them and little time, it seemed, to give to myself.

At the suggestion of my sponsor, I decided to do a retreat. I reserved a cabin on a remote island. It was an old yoga retreat, with a hot springs and a small waterfall, close to a state park with a mountain full of paths to walk. It seemed ideal. I took some time off from work, about four days. I decided to do it during the week as I didn't want to cost myself time from my family.

I went to the cabin. There was no TV or radio. There were no regular distractions. I decided to remain silent for the four days. I read and contemplated. I got up early every morning and meditated. I walked up the mountain at least once a day. I did exercises where I examined each part of my life up to this point. How did I use language? How did I like my work. And what was I going to do in the future? What kind of wife was I and how was I going to change and improve? What was I doing to take care of my body? My mind? My spirit?

I fasted for a day. Then I ate only vegetarian and very healthily. I stayed away from other people and just maintained my integrity unto myself. I got in touch with me again. I liked most of what I found. Some I needed to change. Some I noticed for the first time. I came back from my retreat ready to make things happen in every area of my life. And ready to let things happen as they would.

◆ ◆ ◆

The last areas we may wish to take a look at are the Seven Deadly Sins. We've discussed some of these areas in other contexts and it is worth reviewing those and adding more in looking at some areas that have troubled man from the beginning of recorded history.

The first of these is **pride**. This is number one of the Seven Deadly Sins. Our society is very confused about pride. Religion teaches us that pride goes before the fall. Psychology teaches us that a healthy sense of pride is essential for full functioning in the world. The Program teaches us that the misuse of pride and the misapplication of pride have been part of the biggest cause of our problems. It is no wonder that we have mixed feelings and thoughts about pride.

With all the current interest in self-esteem and self-worth, there is another element to think about when we consider pride. Some of us come from families where we were not taught healthy emotional language and habits. We did not get a balanced perspective of the world and relationships, and some of us got a distorted view of where we stood in relation to the rest of the world. We felt (and many of us still do) *less than*. In order to make up for that we learned to exaggerate and lie and blow our accomplishments way out of proportion in order to feel some value. To succeed, we have to stop thinking we are

less than other people. We tell ourselves we are not
unworthy, inadequate, or unable to cope fully with life's
problems. We begin to see the glass as half-full, instead
of half-empty. We have to get rid of feelings of inability
before we can make progress. As we learn more about
how false pride has held us back from being our full
potential, we remember, "If we change our thoughts we
can change ourselves."

Many of us still think of our value as human beings
is in what we do or in what we don't do, rather than who
we are. It is all about results—the car we drive, the
person we marry, the house we live in, the job we have,
the vacation we take, the clothes we wear. We've shifted
the emphasis from who to what. Taking a look at pride
is gaining a new perspective and looking again at who we
are, not exclusively what we have or do. Some of us have
heard the slogan "the only person keeping us from
having self-worth is ourselves." The willingness to work
the Sixth Step on pride begins by understanding that
having healthy pride in our accomplishments in life is
fine as long as it is coupled with humility and gratitude.
As long as we don't settle for an inferior quality of recovery
and continue to strive for the best, that kind of pride will not
cause harm.

However, pride out of control is dangerous. Too many
are certain they "wrote the book." They take false pride
in their accomplishments and feel they have nothing left
to learn. They are eager to tell everyone how much they
know. This is a sure way of closing a mind that desperately needs to be wide open. This kind of pride has turned
into arrogance that causes many people to "turn off."
False pride and settling for inferiority will accomplish
nothing. We no longer choose to have low self-worth or
settle for *less than*. What value do I have as a human
being? What do I have to offer to others in the way of
service, wisdom, and help? Who have I become, and who

am I becoming, in order to increase my value to the rest of mankind and myself? The thought that must go with us constantly is "How can I best serve Thee? Thy will be done not mine."

We will talk about humility in relation to pride in the Seventh Step. Right now it is important to examine how we define ourselves. What criteria do we use to say who we are? Hi, my name is ——— and I'm an alcoholic. Hi, my name is ——— and I'm a doctor. Hi, my name is ——— and I'm interested in spiritual growth and becoming my potential. How do we define ourselves? That will say a lot about where we place pride in our lives.

Finally, we are reminded that pride is not to be feared. Although it is listed at the top of the list of the "Seven Deadly Sins," but that is arrogance or false pride as we have discussed, not healthy pride which is a necessary part of self-esteem and character growth. To repeat, our Program teaches us that the pride that "goes before a fall" is an unhealthy state, a symptom of character defects of egotism, grandiosity and arrogance.

No harm will come to spiritual growth from the pride experienced when we freely admit to ourselves that any progress of ours was not made by us alone. Humble pride acknowledges the guidance of others and faith in a Higher Power whom we call upon for inspiration and motivation. With humility and God's help, we do learn to have healthy pride in our "good works," progress, and growth in recovery.

The second defect is **envy**. Envy is fear. Just as with pride, envy has a lot to do with results—other people's. We envy the things, jobs, friends, relationships, status and just about everything else that someone else may have. We are taught to envy by advertisers and the media. We must keep up with the Jones. We must live the lifestyle as shown in the beer commercials. We have to have the newest and the best and the biggest and the brightest. We fear we won't get "the good things" and resent when others do.

Part of having things is the believable lie that external things make us okay. If I have all these nice things and stuff, I must be okay, right? So, if I don't have them, something is wrong and I better get moving. Even more importantly, I must envy and feel badly about the people who have what I want. They obviously don't deserve it the way I do. They must be drug dealers or liars and cheaters. Otherwise, how could they have what I want and deserve, and yet I didn't get it and they did?

As we aim toward a lasting and comfortable willingness to change by using the Sixth Step, we find that envy is also a mask for jealousy. And jealousy is combined with other character defects like self-will, dishonesty, hatred, selfishness, and resentment.

Jealousy is a great danger in recovery. The kind of thinking that causes jealousy makes us believe that the world owes us much more than we are able to earn by our own best efforts. To repeat, when we envy others for what they own, for their standing in the community, or for the people who care about them, we are on our way to self-pity. This state of mind produces not only jealousy, reactive depression, and an attitude that "life's not fair," but also anger against the world. Soon, that jealousy and anger turn against those people most dear to us. We are reminded that the Big Book calls jealousy *that most terrible of human emotions*.

Envy is very much caught up in desire. We are taught *desire* rather than *deserve*. Just because we want it must mean we are able to get it, right? The universe operates on a deserve principle—you will reap what you sow—yet we are taught if we just want it badly enough, something will happen so we can get it. No wonder we become frustrated and depressed. Just affirm it enough in your life, and it will manifest. Wrong.

The same rules operate for everyone. We can get almost anything we need in life. We can't get everything we want. We must learn to be selective and to work for what we want. Sow the seeds, and the plants will grow. The more seeds we plant, the more will grow...given proper nurturing, care, sunlight, and water. And, provided we've picked the proper soil. But, we only have time to plant so many seeds. And, God plays a part in the weather and soil. Just like in the Sixth and Seventh Steps, God's part is as important as our part. We must do the work. God provides the environment and opportunity. And the power, and the direction, and the willingness, and the teachers.

If envy is a big part of our life, we take a look at how selective we've been and how we sow. We need to plant the seeds before we expect to harvest. Take a look to see if you are able to celebrate the accomplishments and victories of others. Do we feel good for someone else's triumph? We hope so. That is a big step on the path past envy.

We are reminded of the age old wisdom, "There is not a passion so strongly rooted in the human heart as envy." In the past when we drank, used, or misbehaved, our self-worth was beaten down to the point of feeling inferior to those around us. We wallowed in our character defects of worthlessness, awkwardness, sadness, and self-pity. We were envious of those who had what we wanted.

Envy brought hatred, jealousy, anger, fear, disrespect, and distrust. We wished failure and disaster on people who had become successful or had gained in any way.

Before the Program, many of us wanted what others had, but we didn't know how to get it. Now we're happy with the miracles we receive in recovery. *We have discovered that doing is more important than having and experiencing is more important than possessing.*

The willingness to work on our character defect of envy produces that positive practice of having more compassion, empathy and love.

The next defect is **gluttony**. Many of us have not found a balance point in regards to our dietary habits. Many of us are addicted to sugar...we binge and diet and binge and diet. We have eating problems. We are greedy in our eating habits which effects our health. We've not examined the mix of exercise, nutrition and spirit that is necessary to formulate a plan for living that provides energy, health, strength and endurance. We have sloppy habits of taking care of this temple of the spirit. If we are greedy we are never satisfied.

It is important to put all our habits into the context of becoming *entirely ready*. If we overlook one little addiction or one little bad habit or one little defect, are we just a "little" addictive? How can we claim abstinence if we still hold to other addictive habits and/or character defects? It is important that we realize that the Sixth and Seventh Steps are not just about alcohol or drugs or overeating or gambling or sexing. They are about putting our lives in alignment. **How honestly we work this Step is in direct proportion to our desire for positive change.** No holding back. Please be willing to take a look at it all.

The next habit to examine is **sloth**, which is spiritual procrastination in all areas of our life. We hear that procrastination is the art of keeping up with yesterday. We were constant procrastinators before we began our 12 Step Program. Addiction created the habit of delay because, as long as we had our substance or destructive behavior, everything else could wait.

Now we know that action is truly the magic word. The slogan *Easy Does It* doesn't mean we put things off.

It means to do it, but to do it in our Higher Power's good time. Slow growth, slowly making progress on our defects of character doesn't mean postponement.

We can't put off airing problems to other people for fear of being ridiculed. We need answers early during our progress. When we attempt to ask for solutions, we can be clear and direct in our questions. We know our friends will always give us the right to be wrong and quickly correct faulty thinking. We can work through our character defects just by "pressing on." Procrastination is not living one day at a time. We do today what we are meant to do today. Many of us think we have no problem in this area because we work hard at our jobs. How lazy are we in our relationships? What kind of load do we carry around the house? How about our spiritual practice? Are we carrying our load there? Do we put in the time and effort to grow and expand, or do we just pay it lip service, if that? What about the other areas of our life? Are we continuing to grow mentally, emotionally, physically? Do we practice disciplines and put out the effort to make our time count? Sloth is the thief of time. The character defect of putting off actions "until things get better" is one of the most destructive detours from common sense or staying *right size* we can make. Delays never make problems "go away;" they only make success harder to attain. If we shy away from "bringing out" our problems to others, we are sure to cause stress and misunderstanding.

Quite often, postponing facing up to reality results from fear that others will laugh at us. This is self-pity in action. *Solutions come from direct and specific action.* We always remember that others in our group give us "the right to be wrong," knowing that a change in direction is always possible for anyone with problems. Procrastination wastes precious time. When we procrastinate and delay working our Sixth and Seventh Steps, we are only making sure they will get worse. We remember that solutions come from taking action. Sloth is not just about results—it is about effort. Do we give full effort to everything we do? It is very definitely worth looking at in our lives.

"I'll do it tomorrow" is a habit that leaves us always behind schedule. If yesterday's work is only getting done today, then how can today's work get done? It has, of course, to wait until tomorrow. Can we catch up? No. We are in the habit of procrastinating. We have a black cloud over our head, made up of guilt, anxiety, worry. A feeling of failure creeps in.

In the Program it's *A Day At A Time*. We try to do today's work today. What if we put off the first step of the work? Nothing will give us satisfaction unless we see the value of our day's work. Satisfaction comes from doing the job on time, reaching our goal *just for today*. If procrastination had an effect on only ourselves, it wouldn't be so bad. But no, it puts a strain on those around us. Tight schedules leave little time for conversation or for relaxed meal times, and no time to fit into the family activities. Procrastination tends to lock us out of our community, even the community of the Program. For how can we share when we are in a state of mind which is preoccupied with ourselves and our problems?

Working on this character defect allows us to participate in our personal and Fellowship life. The ability to concentrate, to use our time well, is everything. It is self-control. It's the Program in action. The Fourth Step speaks of instinct gone wild. We must get control of our instincts. When we are tired we have feelings of uneasiness. These feelings come from stress, the strain of always rushing around. But the feeling of uneasiness also comes from an undernourished spirit, a spirit that never has time to go away to a quiet place and rest awhile. Have we not enough in today's own troubles without making a double load for tomorrow?

Benjamin Franklin said, "Do you love life? Then do not squander time, for that is the stuff life is made of." The Twelve Steps are the same for everyone. We are all given the choice, the means to break the habit of procrastination, so we may be free to strive for spiritual growth in our lives.

The next area of examination is **covetousness**. We have a distorted view of coveting in society. Much like envy, coveting (or avarice, or desire, or greed) is cultivated by our advertising and media. We have to possess what others have. We must own and keep and grasp and hold tight all that we can. Examine what is behind it— usually fear.

The other sense of this word is coveting another man's wife or another woman's husband. To inappropriately desire another or a thing is to covet. We covet all the time. It is important to examine this in our lives.

Covetousness brings up questions of ownership versus stewardship; open handedness versus grasping and holding; generosity versus greed and avarice. Where do we stand with these things in our lives? These are very weighty questions. It brings into question our whole view of the world, the people in it and how we deal with them.

Are we greedy? Do we grab and reach and pull and grasp all that we can, at the cost of others and ourselves? Do we value what we own and who we are in a relationship with more than who we are and who they are? Is status more important to us than substance? Are we more interested in holding and obtaining power than in becoming and reaching our potential?

We realize that we are asking more questions than we are answering here, and we think this is an important function of becoming *entirely ready*. We must have a fairly accurate idea of how we view life and how we operate if we are to be in a position to let go of our defects and help in transforming and changing. Most of us do not take the time to closely examine our lives and our manner of living. We make basic assumptions early in life and go on from there, rarely questioning if they need to be changed and if they were effective to begin with. Many of us took the values and methods of our parents at face value (even though we thought we rebelled and changed from them) and find ourselves living very similar lives to theirs. It is important to make sure we know what kind of life we are living if we are to change it. That is why taking the Fifth Step is so important. For that matter, *what a great opportunity the 12 Steps offer us in reclaiming our lives.*

By accepting God's help we learn to think clearly, to play fairly, and to give generously. Our values change in recovery as we become less and less selfish. The value screen through which we see life changes. We no longer ask only what everyone can do for us; we also ask what we can do for them. We no longer only seek out situations that only comfort us; we also discover ways to comfort. We find that we feel better about ourselves when we help others. We learn from our Program that what we may have been searching for our whole lives is wrapped up in service to others.

Our most valuable relationship is the one which creates a closer contact with our Higher Power, so we seek out situations and people that bring us into closer contact.

The values we show in the work of recovery look different from the ones we once held. Every day brings a new opportunity to work on our character defects because our values no longer change with every passing fancy. *Our life now means something and counts for things that are good.*

The next place to examine in our lives is **lust**. Sex, and many issues around sex, may be the most misunderstood and confusing area in recovery. Most of us never learned or were modeled intimacy, so we confused sex with love and lust with desire. For many of us power is an issue in sex and lust, as is self-esteem. All this stuff gets wrapped up and mixed together and called sex or love or making love or intimacy. We usually don't have a clue what it is or what we're doing.

There is much recent research that concludes that many addicted people came from abusive, dysfunctional situations. As strongly as the evidence suggests that genetics plays the key role in determining a predisposition towards alcoholism and addictive behavior, new studies seem to indicate it is how we are treated and shown emotional context and modeling that determines how we move forward. **Although many of us may have come from less than ideal family situations, sponsors remind us that we are working this Step as we are right now, not our families**.

It makes sense that if we never learned to handle our feelings we'd have to find a way to get by—drugs, sex, alcohol, or something. If we came from a family that denied, kept secrets, shamed, repressed and suppressed, physically, emotionally, or sexually abused us, or any number of other ways of creating distortion in emotional, physical, and sexual responses, odds are our sex life is goofy, and has been for a long time.

Many of us confuse having sex with being intimate. Many of us think that being accepted sexually is the same as being loved, only to be disappointed again and again. Many of us use sex to act out our aggression and hate of the opposite sex, in many different acts and obsessions. Men, in particular, seem to be drawn toward pornography and can have very active fantasy lives with very little contact with reality.

Again, advertising and the media have molded and shaped our perceptions of what is and is not a normal love life and how people relate to each other. If we grew up without a good model for intimacy, we may think the **junk** we see on TV and in the movies and in the print ads is how people really relate. If so, we are in for a long and confusing journey.

Lust, and all the areas associated with love and sex, is an area we need to closely examine in the light of our spiritual values. What do we really think of other people? Are they objects, to be used and discarded, to be fondled and played with? Or are they people, with feelings and hearts and depth, to be cherished and nurtured and honored, just as we would wish to be? How do we treat the people we love? Warmly and openly and with respect? Or as badly as we wish, since, after all, we love them and they love us—they have to put up with us?

It is natural to have sexual drives and desires. It is part of being a spiritual being to express love through the body—openly, affectionately, passionately and freely. In light of those spiritual values, it is important to examine monogamy (with sexually transmitted diseases being fatal or permanent now, it also is prudent to practice safe sex, under all circumstances) and all the aspects of being a sexual, spiritual person.

We are reminded what the Big Book (p. 69) says about sex. "We asked God to mold our ideals and help us to live up to them. We remember always that our sex powers were God-given and therefore good, neither to be used lightly or selfishly nor to be despised and loathed."

What comes from our Higher Power is to be honored and treated with respect. Our sexuality has unlimited potential for good. We have so often turned this power in on ourselves and been destroyed by it, or allowed it to destroy others.

The Sixth and Seventh Steps let us change our

feelings about sex so that these new feelings can encourage wholesome relationships. When we walk with our Higher Power, our self-will doesn't run riot over our sex lives. Our spiritual awakening washes over all our relationships, even our most tender and personal.

Working on our own shortcomings allows us to gain a new sense of respect. We learn we can indeed love deeply. We find that sexuality is a powerful, life-giving force that enriches, bonds, and commits us to a special person. We no longer have to face remorse and guilt from uncontrolled self-driven lust. May we rediscover the joy in our God-given sexuality by treating ourselves and others with honor and respect.

Being spiritual does not mean being celibate or chaste. It may include that for different reasons and practices, but our body is as holy as our spirit and can celebrate the gift of love just as fully in harmony with all aspects of the spirit and love.

We need to look closely at how we relate to people. Do we dislike the opposite sex? Do we fear or hate our own sex? How do we identify ourselves as a sexual being? Once we are in a relationship with someone, does our behavior change and we quit trying and showing our feelings and giving fully? Do we honor and respect the other person and the relationship? Once again, the more we know about our ways of dealing with the world and the people in it, the better we will be able to become "entirely ready."

Peter shares this observation about relationships and recovery:
My first sponsor was a very interesting guy. He'd been around the program a while, was a hard driving businessman, and was used to living fast and loose. He'd been married a long time to the same woman, and had some pretty sexist ideas. He and another guy and I used to go to meetings with each other a lot, worked

together, and saw each other socially, sometimes with our wives.

My first sponsor used to go to Las Vegas pretty often with his brother and his dad and my other friend. When they were in Vegas they would do business with prostitutes. None of them saw this as cheating on their wives, as it was a "professional" relationship.

It got me thinking, however. When I got up on my high horse and judged my sponsor for his behavior, how was it that much different than my reading "Playboy" and looking at lingerie calendars. Was it that much different between rationalizing a "professional" relationship and rationalizing a magazine or calendar? Wasn't it still making a sexual object out of a human being and demeaning my current relationship? What was it doing to me and my current relationship with God?

I really had to ask for help to become entirely ready so I could let go of my attitudes and beliefs around sexuality and love that were sexist and belittling and not in line with my spiritual values. I want to be in line with my values. I must ask for help.

◆ ◆ ◆

The last "deadly sin" we will look at is **anger**. Anger is a difficult emotion for a lot of us to deal with because of how we were taught to deal with anger as children. Since it was not possible to show our anger toward adults, many of us have learned to deny, repress, substitute, and suppress anger. Many of us have carried this into our present situations. We never saw ourselves as angry people. We were "intense" and occasionally we'd get mad. But, we certainly didn't see ourselves as angry.

One of the many program slogans says *anger is but one letter away from danger*. Many of us nursed long-standing resentments. Every time we thought about them, we got angry. What makes anger so dangerous is that it burns without consuming. It feeds on itself until it overwhelms all other emotions. *Anger is poison.*

When anger takes over, it acts with uncontrollable rage. We say things, feel things, and do things way out of proportion. Anger is emotional drunkenness.

Because we are in recovery doesn't mean we won't get angry, but the Sixth and Seventh Steps give us a process of working through anger. We learn that what usually fuels anger is fear and guilt. We can dissolve anger. The remedy for fear is faith, for faith means courage. When we are ready to replace our anger with faith, the fear and guilt that cause the anger is worked through, and the anger is removed.

Courage is what makes us do the right thing even when nobody else is doing it. We can find happiness while surrounded by darkness; we can be more loving in the middle of hate and envy, and serene when surrounded by chaos, fear, and anger. The ideas of the Sixth and Seventh Steps help us face impossible odds. We learn that any act of courage may produce future victory for ourselves and others. The courage which we want takes its strength from faith, not from bravery or physical strength. *Let truth and faith, let our readiness and humble quest give us courage, so that when fear knocks, no one is there.*

One word often heard in group discussions is "willingness." Yet, the willingness to do something cannot exist without the action required to do it, and that takes courage. Courage to build our character. It is courage that turns possibilities into realities and assures us that progress in improving our character is possible. Experience teaches us that courage keeps our character defects under control.

When courage guides our willingness, we can be sure that we will not only be capable of accomplishing success, but we are worthy of it. When we know that a goal is worth going for, courage has judgment and carefulness as allies, even though we may be moving against the tide of popular opinion. **Many of the people we come into contact with in our lives who don't live by any Program or belief think our 12 Step way of life is trite, and full of pollyanna slogans and ideas. We can't be concerned with opinions about our way of life, even if others think its trite, because this way of living life has become our secret to life.** We overcome our fears about setting and working toward goals. It helps us to remember *courage is fear that has said its prayers*.

The fact is, that underneath all the denial and rationalization, most of us were in a constant rage, seething. For many of us in recovery, we carry a huge load of anger without realizing it. Many of us stuff anger away like "putting hungry dogs in the basement." Sooner or later, we open the basement door to express a little anger, and out slip the hungry dogs. We move into a rage out of all proportion to what triggered the anger. And, most of the time we don't have a clue as to what happened.

Anger is a common defect in our attitudes and personalities. Like all other character defects, anger grows more harmful the longer it is contained within ourselves. Unless we expose it freely for others to see, it can consume all our good intentions. We must "get the monkey off our backs before it reaches our throats."

How can we possibly make peace and form worthwhile relationship unless we bring anger into the open by working Steps 6 and 7? Letting go of hidden anger and returning to a stable state of mind is one of the first actions in finding a much more comfortable and acceptable peace with life.

We find that "letting it all out" through the 6th and 7th Steps is the way to become freer and happier. We continue to take daily personal assessments of our spiritual growth by monitoring our anger. The old truism when we become angry "to count to ten" helps us to practice the letting go process of the 6th and 7th Steps and become better suited in dealing with anger in an appropriate way.

Anger and fear are closely tied together and many of us in the Program learned to handle our fear with booze and drugs and food and many other mood altering behaviors. Now that we are in recovery, we have to learn new ways of coping with fear and anger. And, we need to learn healthy ways of expressing anger.

One of the biggest risks to a person in recovery is *self-righteous anger*. We become very dangerous to ourselves and others when we are "right." Being right used to mean a free check to treat a person who is "wrong" any way we chose. Especially if we loved that person, it meant we could really cause havoc in the name of being "right."

Most of us never learned that "right" doesn't mean exclusive. There are many ways of being right. We just assumed that there was only one way. We were taught that by our parents, the churches, and schools. As we move into our birthright as spiritual beings, we discover that "right" is a cage, not a freedom. Being right is a perspective, not a license for angry behavior. Each of us has a unique perspective, thank God, and therefore a unique way of being "right." We must learn to temper our anger based on self-righteousness and learn to open our minds and hearts to different points of view. It doesn't mean we won't get angry. *It just means we won't hurt others so often with our "rightness."*

In looking at anger as a character defect, it is important to realize that anger is a legitimate emotion. To deny all anger in the name of spiritual growth is as unhealthy as being angry all the time in the name of being right. We get angry. We need to learn how to express that anger in a healthy, non-damaging manner.

It is the inappropriate expression of anger and the out of proportion expression of anger that is a defect and causes us and others harm.

It was at a meeting that we heard an old timer say, "I am punished by my defects of character, not because I have them." Newcomers can be puzzled by that comment for a long time. How could we be punished by our defects? Then, it dawns on them. God doesn't need to keep a watch on me and note my defects—my defects keep me from becoming all that I can become and limit my ability to grow. Joe McQ. reminds us, "When we have taken the first Five Steps, it is at this point that many people make the mistake of turning it over to God and expecting God to apply Steps 6 and 7 to their lives. But these are our Steps—God doesn't need to take Steps Six and Seven. We do." Lack of power is our dilemma. Anger (and the other 6 sins) keep me from God. Without God we lack the power to live.

Another view of that is the story about Buddha talking to some of his students about anger. Buddha said anger is like picking up a burning coal with the intention of throwing it at another person. We are the ones who gets burned in the process.

Let's take a look at Joe's story:
Before my recovery began, five years ago, the Seven Deadly Sins accurately described my basic character. After my last drink, I discovered to my amazed awakening that the Seven Deadlies accurately described *human nature*. Were Steps Six and Seven going to change my basic human nature? I doubted it. So it took me four years to get to the Seventh Step prayer. But then I was in for some surprises—seven of them.

Slowly, very slowly, at a caterpillar pace, I realized (I love Program realizations) that God is in the transformation business. Before I was even fully aware of it, a change was taking place in my behavior.

As a drinking author, I took great pride in my work. My pride far surpassed my accomplishments. My ego was always fatter than my bank account. Through recovery, I have learned to write what I like and to like what I write. I no longer reach for the proverbial brass ring or yearn to write the nation's next best-seller. I have lowered my sights and have found my true niche. I am content. And I like myself more this way. Surprise! Step Seven has changed pride into self-esteem.

Did I mention yearning for literary fame and fortune? Well, I never worked toward such a goal. I wrote for money. My sole motive was personal gain, no more, no less. Today, I write from a new heart, with the reader's mental and spiritual welfare in mind. Surprise! Caring and sharing have replaced selfishness.

When I was a drinking drunk, I firmly believed that lust was a natural part of the human makeup. I often wrote highly of it, using acceptable euphemisms like "eros," "passion," "fervent love," and "burning desire." It wasn't until sobriety and my third marriage that I could—rather that "respect," "trust," "adore," or "obey"— "be true" to a loving woman. My grandiose ego is far less grandiose. I now enjoy what I once thought was a contradiction in terms: moral sex. Surprise! Love has conquered lust.

Anger was my middle name. Getting even was the name of my game. My bywords were "I'll show them!" and "Who do they think they are?" and "They aren't going to get away with that!" This violent need to punish others blinded me to the rights of others. Sober, I learned that all people are as human as I am and no more deserving of my self-righteous anger than I am of theirs. Surprise! Anger has given way to tolerance.

I was a glutton for everything sensual, including the "pleasure" of intoxication. As it turned out, I was really a glutton for punishment, drinking anything from beer and wine to whiskey and (on one pitiful occasion) aftershave lotion. I wanted more of everything in sight, no matter what it was. I was worse than an underprivileged kid let loose in an unguarded candy store. I was an insatiable sponge. Today, thanks to Step Seven, I no longer pray to have what I want; I pray to want what I have. Surprise! Acceptance has displaced gluttony.

"Don't do today what you can put off till tomorrow." Remember that kind of barroom advice? I do. I lived by it. Even in sobriety, I found myself procrastinating with the Steps, slow to read the Big Book, fainthearted about attending meetings—in other words, dragging my feet. That's why it took me four years to get to Step Seven. Yet, that is when I discovered that I would rather make a meeting than watch TV, that I prefer the Big Book to novels, that I'd rather pray than think. Surprise! The joy of living has replaced sloth.

Today, I understand envy as the incredible sadness that overwhelmed me when others were successful. I was hypercritical and insanely jealous of the "greats," never once looking at the time, energy, and work they put into their success. I simply resented their "good luck," "connections," or "secret." Today, I find myself admiring hardworking people who make it. There was a time, by the way, when I resented the winners in the Program. I now let them serve as examples for me. Surprise! I stick with the winners. Envy in being replaced by inspiration.

Today, I live in a daily state of surprise as Steps Six and Seven work on me. I have surrendered to the spiritual process that removes character defects. Someday, maybe mine will be removed. As I said at the beginning, I move at a caterpillar pace. But that's okay today. As a slow-moving caterpillar spinning my cocoon to the design of the Twelve Steps, I will emerge free as a butterfly. That's a promise God always keeps.

◆ ◆ ◆

We take a look at the part anger plays in our life and how appropriate our expression of anger is. Are we right a lot? Are we upset and judgmental a lot? Are people afraid of us? Do we punish people with our rightness? We look at anger and its consequences. Then move toward being entirely ready to let it go.

It is time now to put this discussion into balance and prepare to move on to the Seventh Step. We have asked a lot of hard questions. We examined some pretty difficult areas of living. We've decided to look for excess in our lives. We are now ready to take action. What, exactly, does that mean?

Can you see why it says in the *Twelve and Twelve* that this is the step that separates the men from the boys? It is gut check time. Are we ready to change our ways of living or not? It is not a "maybe" proposition. It is "fish or cut bait." Perhaps many of us have approached this Step and the one to follow in a less active manner. Odds are we may still be battling some pretty major defects in our life, too. This Step requires commitment and action. There is no better time to get to it than right now.

As we're taught in the Twelve Steps, the chief activator of our defects has been **self-centered fear**. Mainly fear that we would lose something we already possessed or that we would fail to get something we demanded. Living on the basis of unsatisfied demands, we obviously were in a state of continual disturbance and frustration. Therefore, we are taught, there will be *no* peace unless we are able to reduce these demands.

We hear in the Program that F.E.A.R. = Frustration, Ego, Anxiety, and Resentment. We don't want to return to the life we led before recovery, but fear should never be the reason why we don't. Fear keeps us from being open to the Program, from being entirely ready. **If we're**

only in recovery because we're afraid of returning to the old way of life, we'll never pay attention and open our hearts to learn about the new. We'll be too busy looking back over our shoulders to make sure the old life isn't creeping up on us.

We have to want the Program out of a desire for a new life, not out of fear for the old. Positive thinking and behavior will be in charge if we are to make any character growth. Every fear encourages negative thinking that can destroy us. Guilt and shame come from the past, just like fear. If those feelings are what drive us, we will never grow. The Sixth and Seventh Steps let us examine our fears. We learn to take an inventory of each fear until we understand what causes them. Then we will be able to find a way to work through them.

How do we reduce our fears? How do we move into graceful living and growth towards spiritual expression? The answers lie in our ability to become humble and trust—through the Seventh Step.

STEP SEVEN

*Humbly asked Him to remove
our shortcomings.*

The key ingredient in living the Seventh Step is humility. There is not another subject in the Program that causes more confusion than humility. It seems that every old-timer has his or her favorite definition. We all seem to get humility and humiliation confused and many of us have a stereotypical ideal of humility—a spiritual pauper, wearing sack cloth and ashes.

The 12 Step way of life is humble, not in anyway meek. The picture many of us get of a humble person is someone afraid of their own shadow, whose self-image is so low they're afraid to stand up for themselves. We learn that this image of humility is not what is meant in the Program. We realize that the people who have stayed abstinent for some time practice a degree of humility which was foreign to them prior to recovery.

For those who have made progress in their Program, humility is simply a clear recognition of what and who they are. They have gotten down to their own *right size.* Humility is understanding that they're worthwhile. It's the middle ground between the extremes of grandiosity and intense shame. They have a sincere desire to be and become the best they can be. Today we remember that humility is not being meek. It is being our true selves.

Humility for us means staying our *right size*. ***And remembering we are as humble as we are grateful***.

Humility is an attitude. As such, it must be practiced to be maintained, and it must become a discipline to be developed, just like every other attitude. In developing humility we are faced once again with an "active surrender." In asking God to remove our shortcomings, we must move and act in a manner that reflects our willingness and surrender. To do this requires:

+ Spiritual Values
+ Perspective beyond our addiction to alcohol, drugs, food, sex, etc., to the addictive nature of our lives
+ Asking through prayer/willing to receive through humility
+ Trust
+ Understanding the process
+ Responsibility/Action

We will discuss each one of these aspects of the Seventh Step, and hopefully, find a method for making this Step a foundation for the rest of our lives.

The first aspect of the Seventh Step we'll look at is spiritual values. Part of this discussion must be a clearer focus on humility. What, exactly, is humility? The dictionary defines humility as "the state or quality of being humble of mind or spirit; absence of pride or self-assertion" or "acts of self-abasement." Humble is defined as "having or showing a consciousness of one's defects or shortcomings; not proud; not self-assertive; modest." Obviously, the second definition of humble is almost a word for word restatement of the purpose of the Sixth Step: to become entirely ready (conscious). So, if we practice the Sixth Step, humility will result. That seems to make sense, doesn't it? Still, it seems as if something is missing here, and it is important to be clear in this area.

Humility is our acceptance of ourselves. It is strange how we can go to school and learn a lot of facts, but never learn much along the way about ourselves. We can take up nursing, teaching, counseling, giving ourselves to the needs of others, while never having our own needs met.

Why does it seem as if it is easier to solve the problems of the world than to solve our own problems? We simply don't know ourselves very well. When we look into a mirror and attempt to understand ourselves, our conclusions about what we see are usually very different from what a friend sees. When we finally work the Sixth and Seventh Steps, and take the time and make ourselves a priority, we usually make a startling discovery. There exists within us at all times a Higher Power that is the builder of all successes and our comforter during times or trial.

Many of us believe the understanding of ourselves is in direct relation to our understanding and contact with our Higher Power. The image we see and the identity we have is then one of humility before that Power. Humility is our acceptance of ourselves based on our continual surrender.

An aspect of humility that is often talked about at meetings is that of being teachable. If we are humble, we are open to new ideas and news ways of seeing things. Open-mindedness is a very important part of humility. We don't know it all. There is still more we can learn. And maybe even more important, some we need to unlearn. Yet, how many of us in the Program aren't open to new ideas and thoughts? Especially after having been around awhile, how many do we see who continue to say and do the exact same things year after year? It seems that many of us resist a clear idea of humility so we don't have to conform to it.

This is a good illustration of how humility worked in Joan's recovery:

W hat is it about Step Seven that causes so much confusion and apathy? How come we can be in the Program for years and still not have a good idea what the Step means? Are we so blinded by pride that we can't see the beauty of humility and the benefits of this Step? Who needs humility, anyway?

The idea that I might need humility is not a new one. Even during the years of my active addiction, with the lying and bragging, it was not all that uncommon for someone to tell me to *get real* (not a bad working definition for humility, I think). After I started in recovery, my sponsor was fond of pointing out that my way was what landed me in so much difficulty—maybe it was time to look for another way.

The word "humbly" just is awfully hard to swallow for me. Besides that, there is something else that made Step Seven an obstacle for me. It calls for yet one more contact with God—and one that is open and willing for change. This is not just about having an attitude or being ready. This is about being serious about change and doing something about it. No wonder we avoid dealing with this Step.

In the process of working the First through the Sixth Steps, I gained an ability to move through my fear and look toward God. I learned to talk honestly and openly in meetings and to share my limits and fears with another human in an inventory. With the Seventh, however, the situation is different. It is suggesting since I've done the groundwork that now is the time to "humbly" ask to change those things that stand in my way.

I was very afraid of approaching God this way. I don't know why. After all, this is the God who saved me and let me move into the Program and begin a new life. Why was I balking? I had to stop in the middle of working the

Seventh Step and do a mini-inventory. I found that I had relapsed into an old form of pride. I was angry with my inability to work out my shortcomings on my own! I knew I had to relearn that if I stuck to my way of thinking and doing, I was doomed to repeatedly hooking in to my shortcomings. I had to *get real*.

I have heard so many of my fellow members in recovery talk about how they had a religious upbringing, but had abandoned it during their active addictions, and how hard it was to even investigate a spiritual life again. I, too, was brought up in a very religious environment, and have had to set it aside to reconnect with a new reality. My background also included a good dose of the work ethic that I was to be self-reliant and a self-starter. If it could be done, I could do it.

Between these two forms of teaching, I became convinced that life was manageable, and that with enough hard work and a proper religious attitude, my life could even be rewarding. Boy, was I in for a surprise. I had no openness of mind, no emotional or spiritual perspective for growth, no awareness that it could be any different.

When I became willing to start looking at these issues in recovery, it was from a much different viewpoint. It shouldn't have been surprising that it was difficult to develop humility given the circumstances, but it was. I was used to arrogantly demanding spiritual enlightenment or groveling melodramatically for forgiveness. It was a whole different way of being to move toward humility. Gentleness and patience were new to me.

Thank God that by working through the Steps and opening up to any amount of humility I was capable of, things began to change. Humility became a goal and a quality, rather than an obstacle and an obnoxious trait. I've come to know the Seventh Step as an action Step that moves one into humility. By asking, we become humble and the more we ask and open up, the more humility we can receive. These are the ideas that lead me into the area of God-readiness and the ability to change and grow—by asking.

◆ ◆ ◆

Another part of humility is represented in service. Over and over again, we are told that through service we will enhance our recovery, while at the same time helping some one else. By focusing on the needs of others as they see them, we respond in a way that is useful and helpful. **In responding to the needs of others as we would have them respond to us, we superimpose our values and our way of living on theirs.** We see value in giving *our* way. We don't understand why it isn't received in the same manner. We aren't practicing humility.

It is said that in about the same degree as we are helpful, we will be happy. The service work we are called to do in recovery is a result of our spiritual awakening. When most of us thought of service, we thought of restaurant help, chores around the house, washing windows. The thought of service was burdensome if not downright irritating. We probably schemed throughout our lives to do as little service as possible. Every moment we gave to someone else was one less we could spend on ourselves. This stands to reason, for we were totally self-centered. Even those of us who "acted as if" we cared normally received much more than we gave.

The message in the Sixth and Seventh Steps produces *other centeredness*. We, by the grace of God, care less about ourselves and more about our fellows.

When we pass on our recovery, we keep it. This spiritual paradox becomes an all-determining reality for us: to keep what we have found, we must give it away. Service becomes a way of life.

It is suggested that it might pay to re-evaluate our

Twelve Step work and other service work in this light. What is truly humble? Is it being open to learning from those we serve? Or, is it assuming that we have the better way to give, and if they don't receive it, well, we're still sober, so it was a good experience? This Step requires us to look very closely at those values we hold and how we model those values to others.

If humility, being humble, is valuable to us, then we must learn to model it. Practice humility. We do the Sixth Step by surrendering to becoming entirely ready and conscious of our defects and shortcomings. Then the Seventh Step becomes natural.

What other values, spiritual and otherwise, do you hold and how do you model them? Have we examined closely the meaning and purpose of our life? The Sixth and Seventh Steps are really asking us "What is important to us?" And, "If it is so important, where does it show in our life?" Here is where we have to get to the basics. It is easy to avoid this and think we've worked the Steps, but if we don't look closely at the meaning and purpose of what we're doing, the whole context of our action loses its value.

Hard questions, just like in the Sixth Step. What is the value in our life? How is our life giving meaning to others? Are we helping? Are we part of the solution or part of the problem? How does it show? How is our Higher Power part of our life and how does it show? What value do we give to spirituality and how does it show? From the answers to these questions comes our ability to share, to give, to act, and to practice humility.

Let's look at Sam's experience:

I have learned from experience that staying abstinent and attending meetings through painful times is a guarantee of personality change. We no longer have to escape our pain through using. The Program has given us a precious tool, humility, which, used regularly, will transform pain into growth. Armed with humility, we who once dreaded change as much as death can learn to face real life with a new courage and hope.

Before I entered the Fellowship, I lived in a fantasy world of my own creation. I attempted to control not only effort but outcomes of situations. I tried to keep myself calm with chemicals and food, with no recognition for the ups and downs of daily living. *I was seeking an unreal world of complete security, romance and approval; and the more I tried to control (demand) these things, the more chaos I created.* It becomes clear to us in getting sober that we have to change. I like what Bill W. has to say about these rude awakenings in this passage:

"As we grow spiritually, we find that our old attitudes toward instinctual drives need to undergo drastic revisions. Our demands for emotional security and wealth, for personal prestige and power all have to be tempered and redirected. We learn that the full satisfaction of these demands cannot be the sole end and aim of our lives. We cannot place the cart before the horse, or we shall be pulled backward into disillusionment. But when we are willing to place spiritual growth first—then and only then do we have a real chance to grow in healthy awareness and mature love." (*Twelve and Twelve*, p. 114)

Humility seems to be the basic ingredient for transforming pain into growth. In Step Seven of the *Twelve and Twelve*, humility is defined as the "perspective to see that character building and spiritual values have to come first, and that material satisfactions are not the purpose of living." We learn that an honest desire to seek and do God's will is necessary for humility.

"What an order. I can't go through with it," used to be my initial reaction to growing through the Steps. I could accept solutions intellectually, but when it came to practical application, I had trouble. I know today that I don't have to do it perfectly; it takes time to get better. I know that I don't have to do it alone; that I have a wealth of wisdom and support in this Fellowship at my disposal, and that gives me hope for changes, growth, and new frontiers.

◆ ◆ ◆

The next aspect of the Seventh Step we'll discuss is that of perspective.

Bill W. addressed this issue of perspective in a very famous Grapevine article in the fifties about "emotional sobriety." He was afraid that many people were missing the point of the Twelve Steps by focusing so narrowly on the addictive practice that brought them to the pro-gram—in his case, alcohol. As it points out in the Big Book, alcohol (drugs, sex, food, gambling, etc.) is just a symptom. The underlying disease is much more subtle and insidious than the gross outer behaviors might suggest. It raises the question of what the addictive behavior is masking. Those in recovery must be doubly on guard against compulsive behavior and mood altering through habitual activities or substances.

In light of what Bill W. said about emotional sobriety and the symptom of the disease, it is imperative that members open their perspective to a larger view.

The nature of the Seventh Step asks us to humbly be willing to let go and practice what we learned. If we must defend a lifestyle that appears to be unhealthy and addictive, are we being humble and willing? Where else in our lives are there addictive patterns?

Those in recovery have to be very careful to be willing to grow and change and move past old habits of relating and to put new spiritual values into their lives. How are the relationships in our life? What patterns have you developed and how are they changing now? Are we willing to examine that part of our life? And to ask for help in changing it?

Here is an example from John:

Humbly asked who? To remove what? Shortcomings? What are they? It seems as long as I kept asking these questions, even after getting answers from my sponsor, reading, friends, etc., I didn't have to "take" this Step. It's like asking the question "Why?" *Why* is the unanswerable question for me. Just like little children when they ask, "Why?" When they get the answer, they ask, "Why?" again and again, and so on. I used the question like a hold off on Step Seven.

The fact is that when I took this Step on one of my shortcomings—false pride—it gave me the opening I needed to continue to use this Step as another "self-knowledge" step (like Four and Five). Step Seven has the power of disconnecting from "old self." Certainly, I have admitted my powerlessness, unmanageability, dishonesties, and childlike behavior, but they had become so much a part of me that I felt threatened to have these things removed. In fact, I considered my over-reacting as a part of me that was useful or at least it was "just me" and people would have to learn to accept that about me.

It's funny now, but as I received the knowledge of self, I realized that I had created the John R. Construction Company, and my specialty was walls. In a wink of an eye, I had walls erected that could keep out anyone, anything—even God. I had to file a "bankruptcy" notice and go through the process of surrendering all my shortcomings in order for me to get on to living without the safety of my old shortcomings. Certainly, I have still got some, but they are usually located in my "pride locker;" and when I am capable of an honest, humble reawakening, I will report my status to myself, my home group, or friends in the fellowship. Of course, it is impossible for me to do that without giving it up to my Higher Power.

So I stop building walls, make decisions, and act as if I want to be happy, serene, sane, and go on trying to carry the message of spiritual awakenings. Knowing now that the best way to stay away from removing my own short-comings is to accentuate my good characteristics and be honest about what is really a human limitation, not a character defect. To keep uppermost in my mind and heart all of those things that keep me from God stems from pride, mental laziness, dishonesty, and procrasti-nation. ***My staying right size is in direct proportion to my gratitude for the life I have in recovery.*** Thank God He is working on them now. If He wasn't, I would not have written this.

◆ ◆ ◆

Looking beyond our addiction of choice to other areas of our lives allow us to see the addictive patterns in a lot of what we do and feel. Being willing to gain a new perspective is a large part of gaining humility and realizing that there may be much more to our difficulties than drinking and drugging and all the rest of it. We have a disease that affects our life. We need to be willing to see that, and to go forward with changing it. With our Higher Power's help and with awareness we can move closer and closer to our true potential as spiritual beings.

A new perspective can also be called the "surrender attitude" as related by Nancy:

A few years ago I made a very fortunate discovery while going through a very difficult period in my recovery. As a result of this discovery the Seventh Step became my way of dealing with the everyday business of living. The emotional impact of this discovery was very much like having a spiritual awakening. The feelings of exhilaration persisted for several weeks.

For a while, I'd been working myself into a near collapse over my inability to handle my financial affairs. I make a good income, I know there is no good reason for running out of money, yet time and time again I would overspend and borrow to make up for the deficit and run my charge cards to the limit. Of course, this particular time was not the first bit of despair I had felt about my money handling habits. My careful budget and intentions to stick with it "this time" proved fruitless.

I was very unhappy and discouraged. I felt inadequate and doubted my ability to manage my life and move ahead. I was becoming more and more desperate. Then, out of nowhere, came the thought that I was dealing with a serious character defect. I don't know why I hadn't seen it that way before, but I hadn't. I felt sure I could handle it on my own. Seeing it in the light of a character defect put a whole new spin on it. I knew I had better turn to God for help.

I was by myself at home, so I did what Dr. Bob, AA's co-founder, always counseled newcomers to do. I fell on my knees and said out loud, "God, I need help. I can't handle this by myself." Almost immediately I felt a sense of relief and hope. My mind began to clear and I started having some good ideas about how to get myself out of the financial mess I'd created. Soon, I was able to put some of those ideas into action. Weeks later I'd developed methods for keeping myself from falling into that financial sinkhole again.

A couple of days after the initial discovery, I remembered two other surrender experiences that happened to me during my early recovery. The first resulted in my whole-hearted acceptance of the Program and having the compulsion to drink lifted from me. The second happened later and resulted in the resolution of a long standing inner conflict that would have stood in the way of any possible long term sobriety and serenity.

I saw that the Seventh Step could be applied whenever I confronted a similar situation that seemed hopeless and helpless. Usually it involves my blindness to my
own defects. Whenever I find myself uptight or border-
ing on panic, I fall on my knees (figuratively or literally,
if I can) and ask for God's help. My life is now marked by
a series of surrenders and it has never been better.

As the years have past, I've come to a new and deeper
insight into the workings of the Seventh Step. It is this:
if I were able to retain the feeling and attitude that I gain
immediately after surrendering, life would be a continuous serene experience. I don't always hold on to that
attitude as I move away from being willing to surrender.

Let's call it a "surrender attitude." It is an avenue to
peace and harmony. I've learned that it is not so important what happens to me as it is how I view it. If I can see
through the eyes of the Seventh Step, it all can change for
the better.

◆ ◆ ◆

The next area we'll discuss is learning to understand
our fear. As was stated in the discussion of the Sixth
Step, self-centered fear is seen as the chief activator of
our character defects. It can be stated that many of the
faces of fear are character defects. Many of us tend to
deny and sublimate fear, and it shows up in our lives as
many other things. Here is just a partial list:procrasti-
nation, greed, parsimony, tardiness, over-achievement,
under-achievement, junk food, escape reading, TV, video,
self-pity, indecision, overspending, gossip, lying, smoking, shyness, aggressiveness, bragging, and many, many
more. If it is true that there are only two main emotions
in life, love and fear, then all that we don't do out of love,
we are doing out of fear. It certainly makes one wonder,
doesn't it?

In recovery we must constantly challenge ourselves

to see which emotion we are acting from. Am I giving love? Or, am I acting out of fear? Or frozen out of fear? We must constantly examine our motives and be willing to own and name our feelings. For many of us, it was the un-named fears and the sense of impending doom that haunted us during our active addictive days. Those same feelings, in a more subtle form, may still be active in our lives. The way to get through fear is action—and to ask for help. That is what the Seventh Step is primarily about.

The hardest part of this Step is facing our fear. It may be the hardest part of life. Learning to name our fears and understanding the underlying pain and hurt and frustration that cause us to shun away from living fully and completely is our aim. Seeing the many faces of fear and not denying or suppressing or substituting for it is the healthiest way to change our character defects. Most of us need help to face our fears. Most of us need help to change. That is what humbly asking is for.

The Fifth Step gives us a sense of our fears and the Sixth Step our willingness to let them go. The Seventh Step gives us the means to do it. By moving into humility and action, where we can, and asking for help where we need it, we can give up acting through our character defects. Does that mean that we never act out of fear or anger or greed or lust or any of our other defects? Not at all. What it does mean is that we become increasingly aware of those times we do act "out of character." We become more conscious of our motives and intentions before we act. We choose to see the world differently, therefore we act differently. That is why choosing a new perspective—a larger perspective, beyond addiction—is so important. We must develop vision. **And a willingness to put that vision into action.**

How do we find the fear and anger active in our lives and bring it to an awareness level where we can deal with it in a healthy manner? That is probably the root question for the Sixth and Seventh Step. How do we find our fear and name it, and how do we deal with it once we've found it? The Fourth and Fifth Step have given us a big head start on this, but for most of us, the Fourth and Fifth were anything but "fearless." Now that we have some recovery under our belts it may be time for a new look at our fear.

It is time to become aware of our bodies. Most of us go through life totally unaware of our body and its reactions. We live in our heads and rarely give much "thought" to our bodies. If we want to know fear and anger, we need to know our bodies.

The first awareness to develop is that of our breathing. Breath is directly connected to both the autonomous nervous system and the voluntary nervous system. In other words, we can control our breathing and it goes on automatically when we are not aware of it—unconscious, asleep, or with our attention elsewhere. Breathing is one of the few areas of the body where we can directly affect our feelings physically. It is also a place where we can check how we are feeling directly. It is very easy to verify.

We can think back to the last time we were really scared. Totally afraid. Thinking about the circumstances and how we felt. Now, do we have an awareness of our breathing. Chances are we were breathing rapidly and shallowly, or we were holding our breath. Both are very common reactions to fear. Both are almost universally ignored. If we want to know how we feel, we can check our breathing. If we want to change how we feel, we change how we breath.

When a health practitioner or teacher or someone wants you to relax, what is the first thing they say? That's right, "Take a deep breath." Deep emotion tends to make us breath differently. We can gain awareness that way and we can change it that way.

Erin's story is another example of changed perspective:

As I look back over my last year of sobriety (my seventh), I realize it was my best year ever. It was linked inextricably with the Seventh Step and with the unshakable law in the Universe which says that **what isn't growing is dying.**

Dr. Silkworth pointed out in the Big Book that unless an alcoholic can "experience an entire psychic change there is very little hope of his recovery." "An entire psychic change" is nothing short of continual growth. Growth is almost always uncomfortable for me.

Last year I was frequently confronted with pain and the need to change. I resisted a lot of this change because it is difficult for me. I'm addicted to my comfort zone. When I am confronted with yet another character defect, I usually find pain. I usually try to rationalize the defect away, then try to blame it on somebody else (this one is my favorite ways of denying), and finally I resort to promises that I'll never give this up totally.

Last week, I came up against a defect that took me to that point. So, I decided to go to a meeting. It was on exactly what I needed to hear (funny how that works out)—Step Seven. As I listened to the members of the group share their practical experience with this Step I became increasingly aware that I didn't want to give up this particular defect because I was afraid—afraid of what would become of me, afraid of what God might change me into. What if I didn't like what happened?

When it came my turn to talk, I found myself unburdening my soul to the group. And I shared my first real experience with Step Seven which had happened during my third year of sobriety. I'd been working on Six and Seven for a long time and was getting nowhere with it. My sponsor realized I was stuck and wrangled an invitation for me to talk at a speakers meeting about the Sixth and Seventh Steps. I spent the rest of the week in a panic, knowing I had the words but lacked a true understanding of the Steps because of my fear of change.

The morning of the Friday I was going to speak I was met at the back door of the college where I work. Two of my students were waiting for me with big grins on their faces and an air of secrecy. Part of an assignment I'd given them was to supply examples of poetry in action. They obviously felt they had a good one.

They led me into my desk, where a vase was sitting with a string attached, and floating above the vase was a big yellow balloon. It was a very nice looking arrangement, with a juxtaposition of balloon for flower in the composition. They had written a poem on the balloon. Both of the students were brimming with fun and confidence. Then, they told me to pop the balloon!

I couldn't. I hate to pop balloons! I hate the noise. It really bothers me to see a balloon pop. It scares me. Usually I let out a little screech when it happens. They handed me a hat pin and said, "Pop it." They weren't going to take no for an answer. Finally, I took the pin, put one hand over my ear and closed my eyes. I lunged forward with the pin and heard the balloon pop. I didn't screech.

I opened my eyes and saw an amazing sight. Concealed inside the now disintegrated balloon was a flower. I had no idea how they got it inside the balloon. I felt my eyes fill with tears of joy.

At last I understood the Seventh Step. I am just like that balloon. I am so full of hot air, I am afraid to let God pop the balloon and let the flower out. My pride and fear keep me from discovering my own flower and the flowers of others. That night I shared my story with a roomful of grateful drunks and saws lots of flowers in the room. It was like being in God's garden. I, too, am part of that garden.

I have learned to look at others and see the flower. I

may not always see my own, yet through trusting God and practicing the Six and Seventh Steps I can change and grow. By seeing how my fellow travelers in recovery continue to blossom and grow I can develop faith that I, too, am growing and changing.

The next area that we can gain some knowledge of our fear and anger is through habitual holding spots. We all hold emotions in our bodies in different places. "It was like being kicked in the guts!" "It knocked the wind right out of me." "I feel rubber kneed." "I'm stiff as a board." "My stomach is on fire." "My neck is so stiff that I can't turn my head." All these statements are about physical symptoms of emotional states. Not too many of us take the time to make the connections and to correct the underlying causes.

Frank's comments on stress are helpful:

When I find myself in the grip of emotional stress, I force myself to be outgoing, rather than retreating into isolation. My mind is a terrible place to live. My wonderful daydreams often turn into stressful nightmares. My mind magnifies my emotions and lets my character defects out of their cages. My mind/ego tells me that I'm more in love than I am, angrier that I am, more powerful that I am, and mostly, more miserable than I am. When I let stress push me into isolation, I become prey to what the Program calls *stinking thinking*.

There is only stress when my mind is allowed to work its own way. I need people. I need the Fellowship. I need to humbly ask God for help. When people are hard to find, I use the phone. Stress can cause me to hide inside myself, thinking no one else understands. I need to reach out instead, and share my feelings with God and others who can help.

I have also been helped in dealing with stress by learning when to say "no." My sponsor quoted William James to me, "The art of being wise is the art of knowing what to overlook." The benefit of the Sixth and Seventh Steps is balance, a feeling of being centered. If I lean in one direction, I lose my balance and fall over. I can't please everyone. I can't be everything to everybody. There is a balance these Steps teach me between selfishness and selflessness.

I need to be careful to organize my time, establish boundaries and set priorities. I can't sponsor everyone, be at every meeting, or volunteer for every service opportunity. Recovery is not a stressful race to see who can do the most. Easy Does It. I let myself get too stressed out when I'm not careful in scheduling my time. I have been learning and practicing what are called "refusal skills." I need to learn when to say no. I have the right to refuse requests, to slow down and take time out, to take care of myself.

◆ ◆ ◆

With all the awareness of the stress response and how to deal with it that has been brought to light in the past twenty years, it is still amazing how few people use this knowledge to lessen the stress and other debilitating emotions in their life. How many of us carry anger and fear in our backs and neck? How does our solar plexus feel when we get "uptight"? How is our stomach? Indigestion? Ulcers? Do we get headaches regularly? Do you grit our teeth or grind them in our sleep?

It is important to become aware of how we place emotions in our body and to start releasing our habitual patterns of holding them. Probably the easiest and best method of letting go of fear and anger is through exercise. It not only benefits us through the actual physical exertion, but it also gives us psychological and mental release. The endorphins and dopamine that are released through aerobic exercise are very beneficial. Exercise is a wonderful way to do a moving meditation and to practice spiritually.

Dance, yoga, long walks, martial arts, movement classes, and sports are all ways of getting in touch with our bodies and releasing our holding patterns. Fear is a fact of life. Those people who prosper and grow with their fear are those who move through it. We learn to recognize fear in our body and move with it and *through* it. We do something to release it—physically.

Let's hear from Curtis:

I had a big fear of physical exercise or doing anything about my overweight under-exercised body during the first eight years of my recovery. Yes folks, I waited eight years before I looked at that part of my recovery. My first eight years had been very rewarding in other areas. But I was not practicing awareness, acceptance, or surrender about my physical well-being.

I'm not sure if I had an eating disorder, but I did manager to stay on a diet of donuts, cheese, and crackers. It showed in my physical appearance being so overweight. But I was in denial about being fat, except that I felt and thought I should be wearing a T-shirt at all times with the words "I hate myself" on the front.

It may sound too simple, but I just got sick of it and wanted to have my physical body not be an "issue" anymore. Boy, do I dislike that word "issue." So, in wanting to be entirely ready to do something, to move through my fear, to put this "issue"—like so many others in recovery—behind me, I took action. But not on my own. I make the most progress when I ask for help.

I found three program friends to be my physical well-being sponsors. They were in the fields of diet (Marilyn) and exercise (Todd and Lisa). I learned about food and slowly removed the sugary high fat content foods from my diet. I made a commitment to Todd & Lisa to join a gym and begin working out. And I repeated the often used program slogan, "What you are is God's gift to you. What you make of yourself is your gift to God." And, "Dear God, I have a problem . . . me! Dear child, I have an answer . . . Me!"

Why was I up most of the night before the first day in the gym? Was it shame and guilt, lack of self esteem, fear of other people looking at me? I don't know and knowing the reason really doesn't matter in the big picture. I just went ahead and walked into the gym. But I was also helped by another friend, Phil. Phil's not in a 12 Step program and, as we learn, quite a lot of help comes to us from friends not in recovery. Phil is like many people in the world—kind, helpful, and supportive.

Phil had been going to this certain gym and had been helped by a personal trainer, Tom. So I hired Tom to get me going on my exercise program. This was the biggest help, to have someone guide me gently into a regular workout program.

It's now three years later, and I've lost the weight and workout three times a week. My physical recovery is not an "I hate myself" issue anymore. I worked the Sixth and Seventh Step with the help of my Higher Power and Marilyn, Todd, Lisa, Phil, and Tom. If there is one thing I like to pass on to others about the above experience, it is this: My active, crazy, addictive, using years were just symptoms of something else going on with me. The longer I'm in recovery, the more I realize how different my thinking is from most people. *I am* my biggest problem. The more awareness I have of my being an alcoholic forever, and my tending to be self-defeating, the more progress I make. The more I realize how sick I am, the more my sense of humor grows about my way of viewing the world when I'm alone and how my aloneness gets me jammed-up. I just can't do much by myself. I need God, the Steps, and my friends.

◆ ◆ ◆

After practicing a physical approach, a spiritual and mental approach will be very effective. This is where prayer and meditation, as we discussed in the Sixth Step can be of great help. Prayer is *how* we put our humility into action.

Prayer and meditation are frequently associated with the Third and Eleventh Steps. However, it is extremely important to recognize the place of prayer in humbly asking. How else are we to approach our Higher Power when asking for help, than humbly? Knowing our station in life, knowing where we stand with our defects, being aware of the process of change and growth—recognizing all these factors in our lives makes it very plain that we can use all the help we can get. We get that help by asking.

Gail relates to us about "asking for help":

I heard early in recovery that *fear is the darkroom where negatives are developed*. Unrealistic fear used to haunt me and was behind most of my resentments. Fear used to attack me because I was alone and isolated. I only saw dark clouds over my head and all appeared hopeless and negative. The Sixth and Seventh Steps have made a difference in my being full of fear.

I began to overcome my character defect of unreasonable fear by asking for help, by asking my fellow members and my Higher Power. I learned these two sources give me the support I need. But they are not mind readers. I have to open my mouth and share my struggles. I remember, when I share experiences, I can also be sharing troubles. I have learned to share problems as well as solutions.

◆ ◆ ◆

In the Bible, it talks about, "Ask and you shall receive. Knock and the door will be opened." Most of us never ask. Or when we do ask, it is self-centered and self serving. It is not about self-centered requests for more money or possessions or power. It is about becoming who we can become. It is about progress. It is about serving to our fullest capacity. The humility in asking is very important. If we haven't taken the time to put our lives in perspective and examined the way in which we operate, we will not be aware of those places where we need the most help.

It is our awareness and consciousness that needs to be addressed, not our Higher Power's. If we don't become accountable and responsible, then it doesn't matter what we ask for—we won't get it. A lot of people talk about asking and living in a manner consistent with their spiritual beliefs, yet say they are not where they want to be in life. They never stop to consider that they've given away the accountability for their lives, and the ability to change.

This is the big danger in cults, and it can be a danger in a 12 Step Program. People think that "turning it over" takes away personal accountability. "After all, my life is in my Higher Power's hands. If it is goofy and out of control, it's not my problem. I've done my part. I turned it over." In cults, it is even more insidious. If I follow all the rules and beliefs of the cult, I will receive the benefits of that belief—enlightenment or spiritual growth. If I don't grow or become enlightened, it is because I don't believe "enough" or haven't followed the rules "enough." My life is in the hands of the one true leader (or guru or minister or teacher). I've surrendered to this belief, therefore I don't need to be accountable any more for that area of my life.

It is a very cunning trap. It can happen at work. It can happen with a boss. It can happen in the Program. We must be very careful to stay accountable. Ask questions. Ask your Higher Power. Pray. It is important to question. That is how we learn. Those who say "Shut up and listen. You'll learn more with your mouth closed and your ears open," are sometimes the very people afraid to question their own lives. It doesn't matter if we are new in recovery or have thirty years, we need to question what goes on around us and what is happening in our own life. *We don't let someone else bring us down to their level. We need to be selfish about our recovery. We may in many respects be powerless over people, places, and things but we're not powerless over unnecessary hassles in our lives.* We ask our Higher Power for direction and grace. But remain accountable for the decisions we make. It is by God's gift that we have free will. ***Asking and surrendering are not the same as giving up accountability and choice.***

What do we ask for in our prayer? It seems that a humble prayer would contain a request for an awareness of those character defects that hurt ourselves and others. It would also ask for ways or methods of ridding ourselves of those defects. It might be thankful for all the progress we've already been given and all the gifts in our lives. It might also ask that we be shown ways to provide greater service.

A prayer showing gratitude and asking for help in becoming aware of and letting go of shortcomings which allows us to be of greater service may be the way to work Step Seven. Something like:

God, (or Higher Power,) thank you for the gift of my recovery and all the benefits in my life. Please allow me to be open and grateful for the bounty of friends, family, growth, and much more in my life. Please help me gain an awareness of those shortcomings that hinder my service to others, myself, and You. Please help me find a way to remove those character defects in my life, both the ones I'm currently aware of, and those that I may gain awareness of later. Help me become who and what I may become , in order to give more. Amen.

A gentle, open prayer for help and of thanksgiving surely will help pave the way for change. We don't need to make it a struggle or an epic. It can be a gradual, gentle process. We choose. We get to determine how it will go with our willingness and our humility.

There are a few folks in the Program who don't give much credence to prayer and a Higher Power. Many have been in recovery for a long time and feel the quality of their lives has never been better. They question the need for prayer and asking for help in removing short-comings. It seems that the intellect and will alone can rid man of his defects.

Yet, it seems that for many of these people, there is a dimension of living (joy) that is missed. Even the most sophisticated of physicists are seeing that the underly-ing principles of the universe may be mystical and spiritual. The whole basis of life and reality may be nothing more than energy of thought. Maybe God's thought. If this is so—or even a remote possibility—don't we owe it to ourselves to explore the potential of our spiritual natures as completely as possible? Isn't practic-ing and working with prayer a way of showing our commitment to the Program and increasing the depth and width of our recovery? Doesn't belief have to precede the action?

These are very interesting questions and ones which are at the heart of working Steps Six and Seven. Are we willing to become aware of our defects and ask for help? Pretty fundamental, isn't it? Yet, many of us are not ready or willing to do "too much" in working these Steps. It is easier, and maybe more rewarding in the short term, to do another inventory and Fifth Step. It is more fulfilling and satisfying to get on with making amends. Yet, if we don't give our full effort and attention to these Steps, we may miss an opportunity to change the whole way we experience life.

Asking through prayer is a simple and direct way of putting our intent into action. **Are we willing to change?** Or, do we want to hold on to the old ways of doing and being?

It is at this point, where we've made the decision to be entirely ready and to humbly ask, and have put into action what we can and are acting "as if," that most of us let the Sixth and Seventh Step slip away. We don't trust the process.

Let's hear from Stephen:

This is what I read in one of my recent morning meditations: *God can't help us remove our character defects if we keep practicing them.*

Like most of the rest of the Program this statement is very simple. "Why didn't I think of that before?" I say to myself. The answer is "I didn't want to." In the words of Step Six, the first of the two defect removal Steps, I wasn't ready to think that. I wasn't willing to take yet another flyer into the unknown, that free-floating world of happenings uncluttered by the squirrel-cages of my control. I wasn't willing to trust. I wasn't willing to learn or change. I wasn't even willing to be willing, and that is the first condition of working with God on any problem.

Oh sure, the naysayers say, being willing: that's just another way to say let God have His way. Let God win again. Let God tromp all over you. Turn you into the hole in the doughnut.

Well, hey, I'm certainly glad God did the doughnut-hole trick on my drinking. Since coming into AA I have not had a serious urge for a drink. That desire was lifted from me. Same for the desire to use drugs, but that took more time. That was harder. I had to work at that one. I had to show God I wanted to be drug-free, and I had to ask God for help on a daily, consistent basis, and most of all I had to mean what I said. I had to be willing to be released from that compulsion. I had to be convinced that drug use was not to my benefit. I had to say, "I can't. You can. Please help me."

These days I'm working on the defects of gluttony and lust. These twin slobs follow me about day after day, blubbering for more. "You've given up drinking and you've given up drugging and you've given up smoking," they whine. "So why not indulge us? Why not take your ease with us?"

The reasons why I don't are all the same. Any excessive indulgence opens me up to feeling I can do it all, have it all, control it all, ego-whip the world with my will. And that kind of behavior doesn't work anymore. I have to face the fact that I am not an ordinary guy (how I loved that distinction when I was drinking; how it drives me nuts now). *I know for myself, I don't have built into my system many of the rational controls and stops and guards that other people have*. I just want to go, go big, zoom off the launching pad like a missile when, most days, what is called for is a leisurely biplane trip along the Mississippi. A trip that incorporates the world instead of blowing it off.

The foxhole prayers never worked for my drinking and they won't work for any of my other character defects. I can't ask God to help me overcome my desire for potato chips when I'm finishing off another bag. I can't ask God to help me overcome my lust when I'm giving in to it again. I can't ask for help if I'm not willing to be helped. I've got to do my part in order for God to do His.

◆ ◆ ◆

Trust, in many different forms and areas, may be one of the biggest issues facing us in recovery. We lost the ability to trust ourselves through years of denial, rationalization, and addictive behavior and good intentions with little follow through. Many of us lost the ability to trust others early in life when we were faced with loved ones who professed love, then hurt us—emotionally, physically and/or sexually. We may have been abandoned, in many different ways and in many different relationships. We may have been abused and shamed. We may have perpetrated all those things on others. Trusting ourselves and others, and trusting God, after all we've been through, is asking a lot. Yet, if we are to gain the ability to grow to our full potential through the Program and the Twelve Steps, especially the Sixth and Seventh Step, we must learn to trust.

How do we learn to trust and what are the elements of trust?

Trust, like surrender, has elements of being passive and of being active. It takes action to trust. And, it takes an opening or surrendering to our feelings, to being vulnerable. We talked about these elements at the beginning of Step Six and we've come full circle to discuss them again in the completion of Step Seven. Letting go of counting on results and surrendering to the process is what trust is about. If we've given all we have in being willing and asking for help and put it into action, then our Higher Power will be there to remove our shortcomings and give the help we need. The element of doubt arises because we don't know that we've done all we could to be ready and willing. So, rather than trusting that we've done what we could do, we doubt. Or, we begin to look at ways we don't deserve to change and receive the bounty of the universe and the rewards of letting go of our defects and we begin, at a subconscious or very unaware level, to sabotage our efforts and level of perception.

We gain trust the same way that some old style investment houses get money—we earn it. We gain trust for ourselves by being trustworthy. Isn't that a great word? Trustworthy. It is a very valuable word, and an invaluable insight. We become capable of trusting by being trustworthy. It boils down to our personal integrity. *Our responsible actions.*

All the questions we've been asking ourselves about how we live and relate and think and feel gain focus when we decide on a harmonious way of living. Do I live a spiritual life? Do I live as though I've taken a Third and Eleventh Step? Do I act "as if"? The more our actions come into line with our intentions, the more trustworthy we become. When our actions are out of line, we must surrender to the process and ask for help, and trust that it will be forthcoming. We may not be able to pick the form or method of help. We may not recognize it when it arrives. But, it does come. Usually it arrives in the form of an opportunity to do some work. Or, it arrives in the form of a crisis that might give us a way of seeing things differently.

It is like the old story of the man in the flood. A man, who believed in God devotedly, lived by a river, which flooded on occasion. One spring, the rains fell very heavily and the river began to rise. Soon it was above the foundation of the man's house. A sheriff came by in a four by four truck, offering the man a lift and telling him it was time to evacuate the area. The man refused the ride stating, "God will take care of me."

The river continued to rise and soon the man was forced up to the second floor of his house. Looking out his window, he saw a rescue boat approach. Opening the window, he shouted to them to go away, after they had offered to rescue him. He said, "God will take care of me."

The river continued to rise and the man was forced out of the second floor onto the roof, where he climbed up to the chimney and held on. The river rose to where it was swirling around his legs and torso threatening to tear him away into the rushing water. A helicopter came swooping out of the darkening sky, and started to lower a rescue sling to lift the man out of jeopardy. He waved the chopper off, shouting, "God will take care of me!"

Very soon after the helicopter left, the man was swept off the roof into the raging flood and drowned. Upon arriving in heaven, he was greeted by St. Peter and taken before God. Before God could greet him or say "hello" or "how do you do," the man angrily demanded to know why God had let him drown. After all he had great faith and trust in the Lord. God said to the man, "I sent a four by four truck, a boat, and a helicopter to help you. What more could I do?"

Many of us are like the man with a house by the river. *We don't recognize the help that comes our way every day.* Trust is learning to see the help that is already available in our lives and knowing that more is being provided on a regular basis. We must learn to give fully in our efforts to not "drown" and let go of the results.

So, trust is two fold in nature: 1) learning to trust ourselves by being true to our integrity and giving full effort and willingness. 2) Surrendering to the process and knowing that help is available if we ask and learning to trust that if we don't see the help, it may be that we are unable to see it, not that it is unavailable.

Trust comes through action. By acting worthy of trust, we gain the trust of others and ourselves. **By acting trustworthy, we begin to see the help available when we are out of line with our spiritual intentions and our willingness to change.** This is when we gain a true understanding of the process of the Sixth and Seventh Step, and begin to see the lessons take hold in our lives. The only things we used to trust were the things we were addicted to. When we began to put our trust in the Program and our Higher Power, the destruction stopped and recovery began.

Bob shares his perspective:

Detailed investigations, extended over many years, now enable me to present concrete evidence that there is a worldwide conspiracy among countless individuals who point out to me my character defects. I continually uncover such plots and am becoming better at spotting them in my never-ending search to find others to blame. I'm called an "old-timer" because I've been in the Program over twenty years, actually twenty-seven. But I'm not that old, almost 50, lucky enough to sober up as a young man.

For many years, I've believed the Sixth and Seventh Steps are the most important out of the Twelve. It's funny, the more years I add to my recovery, the more important they become. Here is why:

First off, I've learned a lot about myself and the general character I was born with and developed since childhood. I was born with some physical/mental/genetic or whatever predisposition toward compulsive addictive behavior. Without the knowledge from understanding and working the Sixth and Seventh Steps, I can go to any lengths in any direction imaginable to be compulsive. I've gotten over having a chip on my shoulder about this quirk of nature and don't blame my parents. Even if I had "perfect parents" (which really don't exist), I would have been quite a challenge to them anyway. I tell many newcomers they may have to do some work about their parents, but there is a big trap in blaming them while working the Steps. Its too easy to get stuck blaming our parents *which continues to make the past a reliable source of unhappiness.* Our parents don't work the Steps for us.

I believe what happened in the late 80's was what

some call "recovery spillover." All sorts of new members came in and only "two Stepped the Program." They weren't using and they attended meetings. They wanted to still be in control and went around complaining about their parents, childhood, and relationships. Sure, many of us had terrible things happen to us early on, but we're in these rooms to help each other with the here and now. We can't work the Steps while living life looking in a rear view mirror. In the past, most of us didn't need better families, relationships, or partners. We needed to be better people.

The Sixth and Seventh Steps are there to help us all with our real and perceived thought and feelings about our early years. These Steps shake us into an understanding that what may have been inflicted upon us by God, the world, fate, nature, chromosomes and hormones, society, parents, relatives, the police, teachers, doctors, bosses, and especially friends and relationships, is not so bad that the smallest suggestion we can perhaps do something about it may get us unstuck. *If we stay in the worry tower of our indignation, we prevent the healing of past injuries by constantly licking our wounds (character defects).*

Secondly, I am unquestionably one of the most self-centered people in the known world. I'm not interested in why this exists, just that I am continually aware of this defect of character. I've become so aware of my tendency toward self-centeredness it is now often very funny. A good example is when (of all things) I have to wait my turn in the checkout line at the grocery or hardware store. I always get in the slow line where people are writing checks for $1.37 or talking to the clerk. I instantly start taking their inventory, how dare they make me wait, this self-appointed king of the world. I am as angry and resentful as I can be by the time I'm leaving the store. But thanks to my progress in recovery, I have the ability to quickly shift my thought and feelings. I'm laughing at myself before I reach my car. In the old days, that type of situation would have catapulted me into all sorts of negative self-defeating behavior.

On the way to my car, full of hatred and bitterness, I repeated two words, *my usefulness*. It's a short version of the Seventh Step Prayer from the Big Book (p. 76), which reads "My Creator, I am now willing that you should have all of me, good and bad. I pray that you now remove from me every single defect of character which stands in the way of my usefulness to you and my fellows. Grant me strength, as I go out from here, to do your bidding. Amen."

Working Steps Six and Seven are a constant part of my recovery progress. When self-centeredness takes over in its many guises, I repeat to myself *my usefulness*. When I am balanced, I am useful to myself and others. The Sixth and Seventh Steps remind me daily, *I'm ready to be useful*.

◆ ◆ ◆

The action of the Sixth and Seventh Steps culminates in *dropping the rock*. We let go of those things pulling us down and keeping us from being the most help we can be in service to *ourselves and others*. We trust in our Higher Power and we trust in the process. We surrender what can be surrendered, and work out the rest.

The Sixth and Seventh Steps are where the movement into serenity begins. Through Step Five we've been learning to know a Higher Power, seeing the nature of our addictions, and admitting the wreckage of our past. Now we are ready for **action**. Up to now, it has been mostly internal work. We've stopped our active addictive behavior, but have we changed the way we think, behave, and feel?

It is no mistake that we must do these Steps before

making amends. If we're not willing to change our behavior, then where is the value in an amend? These Steps are action Steps, "down and dirty," to the core of our lives Steps. They require accountability and they require action, two reasons that most people avoid them or make them into "nodders." And after amends, we **keep** working these Steps as we gain more awareness about ourselves.

The longer our time in recovery, the easier it is to fool ourselves and others that we've done these Steps. We need to take a very close look at all the implications of these two "quiet" Steps and become responsible for working them during our entire recovery journey.

Please join in working toward "emotional sobriety," recovery with balance, by taking a new look at the Sixth and Seventh Steps. Then jump into action and surrender, making *positive progress* through a continuing series of spiritual awakenings. We spend less time thinking about changing our character defects. *We mature. We change our character defects*.

◆◆◆

THE ANSWERS
WILL COME
WHEN YOUR OWN HOUSE
IS IN ORDER

SERENITY PRAYER

God grant me the serenity
To accept the things I cannot change;
The courage to change the things I can;
And the wisdom to know the difference.

Living one day at a time;
Enjoying one moment at a time;
Accepting hardships as
the pathway to peace;

Taking, as He did,
this sinful world as it is;
not as I would have it;
Trusting that He will
make all things right
if I surrender to His Will;

That I may be
reasonably happy in this life,
and supremely happy with
Him forever in the next.

SANSKRIT PROVERB

Look to this day,
For it is life,
The very life of life.
In its brief course lies all
The realities and verities of existence,
The bliss of growth,
The splendor of action,
The glory of power—

For yesterday is but a dream
And tomorrow is only a vision.
But today, well lived,
Makes every yesterday
a dream of happiness
And every tomorrow
a vision of hope.

Look well, therefore, to this day.

PRAYER OF ST. FRANCIS OF ASSISI

Lord, make me an instrument
of Your peace!
Where there is hatred, let me sow love.
Where there is injury, pardon.
Where there is doubt, faith.
Where there is despair, hope.
Where there is darkness, light.
Where there is sadness, joy.

O Divine Master,
grant that I may not so much seek
To be consoled as to console.
To be understood as to understand.
To be loved as to love.
For it is in giving
that we receive.
It is in pardoning
that we are pardoned.
It is in dying
that we are born to eternal life.

THE TWELVE STEPS

1. We admitted we were powerless over alcohol—that our lives had become unmanageable.

2. Came to believe that a Power greater than ourselves could restore us to sanity.

3. Made a decision to turn our will and our lives over to the care of God *as we understood Him*.

4. Made a searching and fearless moral inventory of ourselves.

5. Admitted to God, to ourselves, and to another human being the exact nature of our wrongs.

6. Were entirely ready to have God remove all of these defects of character.

7. Humbly asked Him to remove our shortcomings.

8. Made a list of all persons harmed, and became willing to make amends to them all.

9. Made direct amends to such people wherever possible, except when to do so would injure them or others.

10. Continued to take personal inventory and when we were wrong promptly admitted it.

11. Sought through prayer and meditation to improve our conscious contact with God *as we understood Him*, praying only for knowledge of His will for us and the power to carry that out.

12. Having had a spiritual awakening as the result of these steps, we tried to carry this message to alcoholics, and to practice these principles in all our affairs.

The Twelve Steps reprinted with permission of AA World Services, Inc., New York, New York.

RECOMMENDED READING

A Program for You
A Guide to the Big Book's Design for Living
Hazelden (800) 328-9000

Grateful To Have Been There
by Nell Wing
Hazelden (800) 328-9000

The Spirituality of Imperfection
Modern Wisdom from Classic Stories
by Ernest Kurtz and Katherine Ketcham
Bantam (800) 223-6834

The Steps We Took
by Joe McQ.
August House (800) 284-8784

Twenty-Four Hours a Day
Hazelden (800) 328-9000

HAZELDEN INFORMATION AND EDUCATIONAL SERVICES
P.O. Box 176
15251 Pleasant Valley Road
Center City, MN 55012-0176

◥HAZELDEN°

**For price and order information, or a free catalog,
please call our Telephone Representatives.**

1-800-328-0098
(Toll Free. U.S., Canada, and the Virgin Islands)

1-651-213-4000
(Outside the U.S., and Canada)

1-651-213-4590
(24-Hour FAX)

http://www.Hazelden.org
(World Wide Web site on Internet)